THE NEW MIDDLE EAST

WHAT EVERYONE NEEDS TO KNOW®

THE NEW MIDDLE EAST

WHAT EVERYONE NEEDS TO KNOW®

JAMES L. GELVIN

OXFORD
UNIVERSITY PRESS

OXFORD
UNIVERSITY PRESS

Oxford University Press is a department of the University of Oxford. It furthers the University's objective of excellence in research, scholarship, and education by publishing worldwide. Oxford is a registered trade mark of Oxford University Press in the UK and certain other countries.

"What Everyone Needs to Know" is a registered trademark of Oxford University Press.

Published in the United States of America by Oxford University Press 198 Madison Avenue, New York, NY 10016, United States of America.

© Oxford University Press 2018

Library of Congress Cataloging-in-Publication Data
Names: Gelvin, James L., 1951– author.
Title: The new Middle East : what everyone needs to know / James L. Gelvin.
Other titles: What everyone needs to know.
Description: Oxford : Oxford University Press, 2018. |
Series: What everyone needs to know |
Includes bibliographical references and index.
Identifiers: LCCN 2017009576 | ISBN 9780190653989 (pbk. : alk. paper) |
ISBN 9780190653996 (hardback : alk. paper)
Subjects: LCSH: Middle East—Politics and government—21st century. |
Middle East—History. | Arab Spring, 2010– | IS (Organization)—History. |
Middle East—Foreign relations—21st century. | Human security—Middle East.
Classification: LCC DS63.123 .G45 2018 | DDC 956.05/4—dc23
LC record available at https://lccn.loc.gov/2017009576

1 3 5 7 9 8 6 4 2

Paberback Printed by LSC Communications, United States of America
Hardback Printed by Bridgeport National Bindery, Inc., United States of America

CONTENTS

PREFACE   IX

1. Before the Deluge: The Middle East, 1945–2011   1

What is the Middle East?   1

Who lives in the Middle East?   2

What is the Middle East state system?   4

Do the states in the Middle East have anything in common?   8

What was political life like in the Middle East up through 2010?   11

How did state formation in the region breed autocracies in the
Middle East?   14

How did great power meddling in the region foster autocracies in
the Middle East?   15

How has the exploitation of oil affected the Middle East?   18

What is the "New Middle East"?   21

2. The Arab Uprisings and Their Fallout   24

How did the Arab uprisings begin?   24

How appropriate is the term "Arab Spring" to describe the uprisings?   27

What deep-seated factors made Arab states vulnerable to popular anger?   29

What contingent factors made Arab states vulnerable to popular anger?   32

What were the uprisings like in Tunisia and Egypt?   33

What did almost everyone get wrong about the Egyptian Revolution? 35

Why have Islamic movements been so popular in the Middle East? 37

Why were uprisings in Yemen and Libya so violent? 39

How could regimes in Bahrain and Syria hold on so doggedly? 41

Why did the uprisings leave most Arab monarchies relatively unscathed? 43

What were protests in hybrid regimes like? 45

Were the Arab uprisings bound to fail? 47

What were the overall effects of the uprisings that began in 2010–2011? 48

3. The Syria Imbroglio 51

How did the Syrian uprising begin? 51

How did the uprising in Syria differ from the uprisings
in Tunisia and Egypt? 52

What was political and economic life like in Syria before the uprising? 54

Who is Bashar al-Assad? 57

How did the regime militarize the uprising? 57

How did the regime sectarianize the uprising? 59

What foreign assistance has the Syrian government received? 61

Who supports the opposition? 63

How has foreign intervention prolonged Syria's agony? 66

Who is the Syrian opposition? 68

How bad is the damage to Syria? 71

How has the Syrian uprising affected Syria's neighbors? 74

How will the Syrian civil war end? 77

4 The Rise and Decline of ISIS 83

What is ISIS? 83

Where did ISIS come from? 84

What does ISIS believe? 86

Is ISIS apocalyptic? 88

Is ISIS "Islamic"? 90

Why was ISIS able to conquer so much territory so quickly? 91

Who joins ISIS?   94

Where has ISIS spread?   96

What is life in the Islamic State like?   98

Why did the United States undertake military action against ISIS?   101

Why did ISIS begin its global campaign of terrorist attacks?   103

What impact has ISIS had on the Middle East?   105

What does the future hold for the ISIS caliphate?   106

What happens to ISIS once its caliphate has disappeared?   109

5. Patrons, Proxies, and Freelancers: The International Relations of the New Middle East   112

How much did US strategy in the Middle East change
under Barack Obama?   112

What has happened between the United States and its partners in
the region?   116

Did Obama have a strategy for the Middle East?   120

What was America's policy toward Iran under Obama?   124

What role does oil play in the New Middle East?   125

What are the roots of the Saudi-Iranian competition?   127

What is Turkey's role in the New Middle East?   132

Whatever happened to the Israel-Palestine conflict?   134

6. Human Security in the New Middle East   137

What is "human security"?   137

How do population pressures affect the Middle East?   139

What are the effects of diminishing water supplies on the Middle East?   140

What is the impact of war on the environment in the Middle East?   142

How might climate change affect the Middle East?   144

What is the refugee crisis all about?   145

What is the status of women in the Middle East?   148

How poor is the Middle East?   152

What is the state of human poverty in the non–Gulf Cooperation
Council Arab world?   155

What is education like in the Arab world?   158

Can human security be measured?   160

What are the greatest threats to human security in the New Middle East?   162

What might the recent history of the Middle East teach us about the possibility of overcoming the lack of good governance?   163

NOTES   169
FURTHER READING   175
INDEX   179

PREFACE

I am a historian by training and trade. Although I began my career as a specialist in early-twentieth-century Syria, the onrush of events in the Middle East and the insatiable appetite of the general public for information that might help it better understand the region encouraged me to shift my focus to what is called "contemporary history"—a phrase that seems more a contradiction in terms than an established subfield of history. Hence my book, *The Arab Uprisings: What Everyone Needs to Know*, also published by Oxford University Press.

One of the greatest practitioners of my trade, Fernand Braudel, once wrote that anyone who tries to understand current affairs by focusing only on today and the immediate past "will continually have his eye caught by anything that moves quickly or glitters." However (he continued), a knowledge of history enables us "to know whether what one is witnessing is the rise of a new movement, the tail end of an old one, an echo from the very distant past, or a monotonously recurring phenomenon."[1] History matters: it is embedded in the present (or, as novelist William Faulkner put it, "The past is never dead. It's not even past."[2]). And so I wrote this book to apply what I have learned over the years to ongoing events.

I am grateful for the encouragement and hard work of my editor at Oxford University Press, Nancy Toff, and her assistants, Elda Granata and Elizabeth Vaziri. I am also grateful to those who reviewed the manuscript for this book, whose criticisms and suggestions made it all the better. Finally, I am grateful to my students at UCLA who, on multiple occasions, patiently sat through seminars and lectures concerning many of the issues raised in this book while I honed my arguments and put them in a comprehensible form.

Earlier renditions of parts of this book first appeared on the online websites History News Network and The Conversation. I have also drawn from my print publications, including *The Arab Uprisings: What Everyone Needs to Know*, 2nd ed. (New York: Oxford University Press, 2015); *The Modern Middle East: A History*, 4th ed. (New York: Oxford University Press, 2015); and "The Arab World at the Intersection of the Transnational and National," in David W. Lesch and Mark Haas (eds.), *The Arab Spring: Hope and Reality of the Uprisings*, 2nd ed. (Boulder, CO: Westview Press, 2012).

THE NEW MIDDLE EAST
WHAT EVERYONE NEEDS TO KNOW®

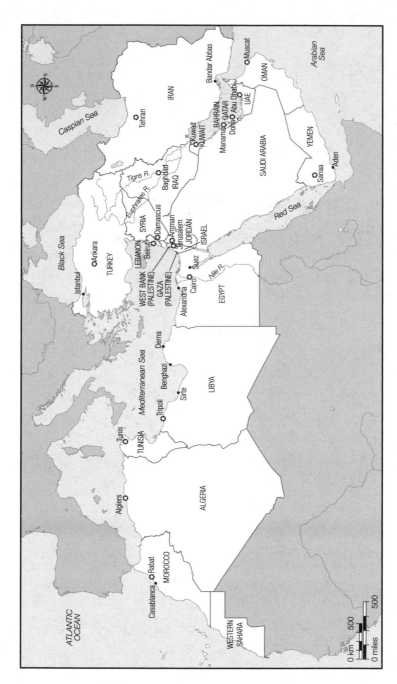

Map 1 The Middle East

1

BEFORE THE DELUGE

THE MIDDLE EAST, 1945–2011

What is the Middle East?

"Middle East" is one of several terms that refer to the territory of southwest Asia and North Africa. Other terms for the same region include Greater Middle East, Near East, and Middle East and North Africa (MENA).

Although now commonplace, the term "Middle East" is of recent vintage. It was coined in the first years of the twentieth century. At the time, it referred only to the area surrounding the Persian Gulf. In 1920, the British Royal Geographic Society recommended its use to refer to the area stretching from the Turkish Straits in the west to the frontier of India in the east. Nevertheless, it did not displace "Near East" in British and US policy circles until World War II. But even after the term passed into general usage, the boundaries of the region remained imprecise and a bit arbitrary. Is Sudan, an Arab state bordering Egypt in the south, part of the Middle East? What about Armenia?

In this book, "Middle East" refers to the territory that stretches from Morocco in the west to Iran in the east. It includes Morocco, Algeria, Tunisia, Libya, and Egypt (but not Sudan—boundaries have to be drawn somewhere) in North Africa, and Syria, Lebanon, Israel, Palestine, Jordan, Iraq, Iran, Kuwait, Saudi Arabia, Bahrain, Qatar, the United Arab Emirates (UAE), Oman, and Yemen (but not Armenia—again, for the same reason) in southwest Asia. It also includes Turkey, which straddles Europe and southwest Asia.

Who lives in the Middle East?

According to the United Nations Population Division, as of 2015 there were approximately 510 million people living in the Middle East.[1] This statistic must, however, be treated with some skepticism. For example, Lebanon has not conducted a census since 1932. Doing so might invalidate the agreed-upon formula for proportional representation among the various religious groups living there. Because of conscription in Egypt, parents do not always register the births of their sons. And although the United Nations puts the population of Qatar at more than two million, that statistic fails to take into account that more than 90 percent of the people living in Qatar are temporary guest workers. There are fewer than 300,000 Qatari citizens.

Whatever the number of inhabitants of the region, however, those who live there represent a broad array of ethnic, linguistic, and religious groups. The three largest ethnic groups are Arabs, Turks, and Iranians. Arabs make up the overwhelming majority (as of 2015, there were more than 345 million Arabs in the Middle East). Most Arabs, Turks, and Iranians live in the Arab world, Turkey, and Iran, respectively. But Arabs, Turks, and Iranians live outside those areas as well. Arab populations live in both Turkey and Iran, ethnically Turkish tribes live in Iran, and Iranian refugees live in both Iraq and Turkey.

Other ethnic groups in the region include Kurds and Berbers. Kurds live mainly in Turkey, Iraq, Syria, and Iran. Clocking in at about thirty-five million, they represent the world's largest stateless nation. Most Berbers live in North Africa. Because the term "Berber" can refer both to those who descend from the inhabitants of the region who lived there before the Arab conquest in the eighth century as well as to those whose native language is Tamazight (Berber), estimates of the number of Berbers vary widely.

The Middle East is also linguistically diverse. The native language of most Arabs and Turks is, of course, Arabic and Turkish, but Farsi (also known as Persian) is the native language of only about half the population of Iran. Other ethnic groups in the region have their own native languages, such as Kurdish, Tamazight, and Armenian. And in Israel Hebrew (as well as Arabic) is the official language.

A majority of the inhabitants of the Middle East are Muslim. There are two main branches of Islam—Sunni Islam and Shiʻi Islam. The split in the Islamic community took place after the death of Muhammad, when his followers disagreed about who should lead the community. Over time, each branch developed different rituals, traditions, and beliefs. Understanding that there is a divide between Sunnis and Shiʻis is important for understanding some of the political rivalries in the region. It is important to note, however, that the rivalries that pit members of the two communities against each other concern political issues, such as which group should govern. They rarely concern religious issues per se. Where sects contend against each other, religion merely acts as an identifier of the political community to which one belongs. Therefore, understanding how each community's rituals, traditions, and beliefs differ from the other's is not at all important for understanding the New Middle East.

Most Arabs and Turks are Sunnis, although Shiʻis make up a significant minority in Lebanon, Yemen, Kuwait, and Saudi Arabia. They make up a majority in two other Arab countries, Bahrain and Iraq. Most Iranians are Shiʻis, and Iran is the world's largest Shiʻi country.

There are numerous other religious groups in the region as well. Christians of various stripes—Orthodox, Catholics, Maronites (mainly in Lebanon), Copts (mainly in Egypt)—live throughout the Middle East. After the establishment of the State of Israel, most of the members of the Arab world's once flourishing Jewish communities quit their homelands voluntarily or because they were coerced to do so by their governments. The largest number decamped to Israel. A similar exodus of Iranian Jews took place after the establishment of the Islamic Republic in 1979. Then there are a myriad of other religious groups as well, including Zaydis in Yemen, Alawites in Syria and Turkey, Alevis in Turkey, Yazidis in Iraq and Syria, Ibadis in Oman and North Africa, and Druze in Israel, Syria, Lebanon, and Jordan. Again, the fact that these groups are present in the region is, at times, an important element in our story.

What is the Middle East state system?

The year 2016 marked the hundredth anniversary of the Sykes-Picot Agreement, and there were countless op-eds and commentaries commemorating (bemoaning?) it. This agreement was a plan hatched during World War I by two officials, Sir Mark Sykes of the British War Office and François Georges-Picot, the French consul in Beirut, to divide up the Asiatic provinces of the Ottoman Empire in the aftermath of the war. The Ottoman Empire, which ruled much of the Asiatic Arab world as well as Anatolia (the site of present-day Turkey) and Egypt, had entered the war on the side of the Central Powers, which Britain, France, and their allies were fighting.

Ever since, Sykes-Picot has come to symbolize the artificial nature of state boundaries in the Middle East. According to most of the op-eds and commentaries, because these boundaries were drawn by far-off diplomats, who had no regard for the wishes of the populations of the region or for the religious and ethnic bonds that united and divided them, we have instability in the region today.

Or at least that is the story. The reality is quite different. The boundaries Mark Sykes and François Georges-Picot drew up would have been no more or less artificial than any other boundaries that separate states—had they actually gone into effect. They did not. The British, whose military actually occupied the territory covered by the agreement, were dissatisfied with the boundaries, and the French were powerless to complain. In other words, by the end of World War I the agreement was already a dead letter.

How, then, did states in the territory covered by the agreement (which, by the way, included only a tiny fraction of the territory of the Middle East) get their boundaries? In the Asiatic Arab territories, a number of states had their boundaries set through the mandates system, which the League of Nations, the precursor to the United Nations, instituted there. The system allotted Britain and France temporary control over territory in the region. The two powers took it upon themselves to combine or divide territories into proto-states in accordance with their imperial interests. Thus, Britain created Iraq and Trans-Jordan (later the Hashemite Kingdom of Jordan, or simply Jordan) after the war. Israel and Palestine came even later. France did the same for Lebanon and Syria.

Those states, like most others in the Middle East, gained their independence during two waves. The first wave took place during the period between World War I and World War II. Iraq, Saudi Arabia, and Turkey achieved independence then, and Egypt became somewhat independent (Iran and Oman—the latter known then as Muscat and Oman—were already independent states). The British granted independence to its mandate, Iraq, mainly because it was a drain on the imperial treasury. They almost did the same for Egypt, which they had been occupying since 1882. After a widespread rebellion convinced them that Egypt would be ungovernable unless changes were made, they granted Egypt "conditional independence" in 1922. It took Egyptians almost thirty-five years to eliminate the British role there entirely and change conditional independence into full independence.

Saudi Arabia and Turkey achieved independence on the battlefield. In the former case, Abdulaziz ibn Saud, a warlord from north/central Arabia, led an army composed of warriors from a mix of tribes that conquered much of the Arabian Peninsula. When the dust had settled, he established a dynasty that has ruled Saudi Arabia to this day. In Anatolia, Turkish

nationalists fought a grueling four-year war that drove out foreigners who had been occupying the peninsula since the end
of World War I. The result was the contemporary Republic of
Turkey.

The second wave of state construction took place during
the Period of Decolonization, which began after World War II
and lasted through the first half of the 1970s. The Period of
Decolonization marked the end of formal British, French, and
Portuguese colonial empires. During this period, Morocco,
Algeria, Tunisia, Lebanon, and Syria gained their independence from France (Spain also abandoned most of the territory
it controlled in Morocco). Much of the Gulf (the UAE, Qatar,
Bahrain, and Kuwait), along with Israel and Jordan, gained
theirs from Britain.

None of these places had been colonies, per se. There had
been only one real colony in the Middle East—the British colony of Aden. After independence, Aden became, first, part of
South Yemen, then part of Yemen (established in 1990 when
North Yemen merged with South Yemen). Instead of colonies, the British and French empires in the Middle East consisted mainly of mandates and protectorates (proto-states in
which local rulers set domestic policy and kept order while
Britain and France handled their dealings with the rest of the
world). There was also the occasional occupation (Egypt) or
the wholesale integration of territory into the mother country
(as in the case of Algeria, which the French considered as much
a part of France as Paris until its independence in 1962). Libya,
which the Italians had integrated into Italy in like fashion, also
became an independent state during this period. Captured by
the Allies from the Italians during World War II, Libya became
a ward of the United Nations, which granted it independence
three years after the organization's founding.

Some states in the region—Turkey, Israel, Algeria—won
their independence through armed struggle. Others—most of
the mandates, for example—won it through negotiation. And
some—Saudi Arabia, Yemen—went through painful periods

before the state-building process was over. Then there is the unique case of Palestine. Palestinians engaged in armed struggle with Israel for forty-five years before joining their opponent in direct negotiations. Short bursts of negotiation, separated by periods of breakdown and conflict, have continued since the 1990s. In the meantime, the United Nations voted to recognize Palestine as a nonvoting observer state in 2012.

In spite of its motley origins and the lamentations of those who hold onto the myth of Sykes-Picot, the Middle East state system has been remarkably stable ever since the end of the Period of Decolonization. There have been exceptions, of course, including the shifting borders of Israel and the unification of North and South Yemen in 1990. Nevertheless, the state system in the Middle East has been one of the most stable state systems in the world. It certainly has been more stable than the state system in Europe.

There are two reasons for this stability. First, the passage of time. Although most member states of the state system in the region received their complete independence after World War II, the process of formulating distinct national identities began while those states were under foreign rule. Ever since, states engaged their citizens in common practices and worked to develop their own internal markets and divisions of labor—necessary (but obviously not sufficient) preconditions for the formation of distinct national identities. The states in the region also jealously guarded their borders, rewrote their histories, and, indeed, produced enough of their own histories to differentiate their national experience from that of their neighbors. As a result, with the exception of Yemen, no attempt to adjust state borders by negotiation—including the short-lived union between Egypt and Syria (the United Arab Republic, 1958–1961)—bore fruit during the postcolonial era.

The second reason the state system has been relatively stable has been support for that system provided by great powers—first Britain, then the United States—and by regional actors anxious to maintain the status quo. Great power intervention has occurred whenever some strongman or national liberation movement has risen to the surface and threatened to upset the balance of power or great power interests. Britain twice intervened in Oman (1959, 1975) to crush rebellions that threatened to divide the country. The British again intervened in the Gulf in 1961 to protect newly independent Kuwait from its northern neighbor, which claimed it as Iraq's nineteenth province. Iraq's Saddam Hussein reasserted that claim in 1990. Once again, foreign intervention forced an Iraqi retreat.

Do the states in the Middle East have anything in common?

At first glance, the states in the Middle East seem as varied as the people who inhabit the region. The Middle East includes twelve republics and eight monarchies. Three states—Egypt, Turkey, Iran—currently have populations in excess of eighty million, while the populations of Lebanon and Kuwait (including guest workers) hover around four million. Algeria, geographically the largest state in the region, spans close to one million square miles. Bahrain, the smallest, includes fewer than three hundred. Then there are the differences in wealth. According to the International Monetary Fund (IMF), as of 2015 the adjusted annual income for each citizen of Qatar, the wealthiest state in the region, was $132,000; for those living in Yemen, the poorest, it was under $2,700. And, considering Yemenis have experienced years of civil strife, that figure now can be only an overestimation.

Nevertheless, beneath the apparent variations among the countries of the region, there are some striking similarities. From the Period of Decolonization through the last decades of the twentieth century, governments throughout the region (Lebanon excepted) played a major role in the economy. They did so to force-march economic development, expand employment opportunities, reward favored groups in the population, and gain control over strategic industries. Governments also provided a wide array of social benefits for their populations, including employment guarantees, health care, and education. In addition, governments subsidized consumer goods.

There were a number of reasons why governments in the region—and, indeed, throughout the developing world—adopted these policies. The United States encouraged them to do so, believing that a combination of economic development and welfare would create stable, pro-Western states. So did international financial institutions, such as the World Bank and the IMF, and a legion of development experts who passed on cookie-cutter policies wherever they went. These policies fit the economic paradigm popular at the time. That paradigm gave pride of place to full employment and rising standards of living as the two indicators of economic success. Governments, it was believed, could guide resources to ensure that both goals were reached more effectively in environments in which markets were not well developed.

The third factor leading to the adoption of these economic policies was the logic of decolonization. Before independence, imperial powers set economic policy, mainly for their own benefit. With independence, governments asserted their economic rights to make up for lost time. They also attempted to win domestic support through the redistribution of national wealth.

To pay the cost of development and their welfare policies, almost all states in the region depended on a type of revenue known as "rent." Rent is revenue that states derive from sources other than taxation. The Middle East as a whole is the most rent-dependent region in the world.

The most obvious source of rent in the region is oil. In 2010, for instance, oil exports accounted for 80 percent of the UAE's revenue, 83 percent of Kuwait's, and 88 percent of Saudi Arabia's. But there have been other sources of rent as well. Egypt derives much of its revenue from foreign aid, Suez Canal tolls, and hydrocarbon (oil and natural gas) exports. Syria has received foreign aid both from countries that want to keep it out of mischief and from countries that want to encourage that mischief. And over the course of its lifetime, Israel's rent income has come in the form of American aid (around $3 billion each year in the form of direct military aid since Israel signed a peace treaty with Egypt in 1979), reparations from Germany for the Holocaust, and contributions and loans from Jews living abroad.

In the Arab world, dependence on rent has shaped the relationship between states and their citizens. Access to rent not only means that the state does not have to solicit revenue from its citizens, it also ensures that the state will be the dominant economic actor. This has enabled the state to attach itself to its population through ties of patronage. It also makes it possible for states to temper or buy off dissent—although, as governments throughout the Arab world have increasingly discovered since the 1980s, loyalty has to be earned as well as bought. Overall, states' access to rent in the Arab world reinforces a relationship between the state and its citizens that can be summed up in the phrase "benefits for compliance": Sit down, shut up, and we'll take care of you.

Just as the norms of the global economic and political systems shaped states in the Middle East from the Period of Decolonization through the late 1970s, so, too, did a different set of norms that spread worldwide thereafter. If the first period was one in which the state was to play an active role in guiding development and providing welfare, the second was one in which the state was to back off and play a minimal role. As the theory went, free trade and a market-driven approach to economics would enable the sorts of economic gains that had proved so elusive under the old system. This doctrine came to be known as neo-liberalism.

Neo-liberalism began as a response to the international economic crisis of the 1970s. American policy makers saw it as a panacea for a host of ills, including the threat to America's dominant position in the world economy and the inability of the overextended governments in the developing world to meet their international economic obligations. The American government therefore pushed rigorously for neo-liberalism wherever diplomats gathered to decide global economic policy. They were assisted in their efforts by the IMF, an organization which the United States dominated and whose job it was to assist countries whose economies had tanked. If those countries needed loans, or if they merely wanted to be deemed creditworthy, the IMF insisted they undertake structural "reforms" to set them on the right path. Only then did the IMF render the necessary assistance.

Neo-liberalism reshaped states, their institutions, and their relationship to their populations. With governments no longer responsible for guaranteeing full employment and social welfare, neo-liberal experts from the IMF and their partners inside governments advised those governments to sell off state-owned enterprises to private investors, reduce tariff barriers and currency controls to promote trade, balance their budgets, deregulate business, and the like. The result was rarely pretty. Popular resistance, corruption, and entrenched interests prevented the realization of the neo-liberal dream in most of the region (if, indeed, it was realizable). Thus, aside from the highly touted winners in the Middle East—Israel and Turkey—the overall effect of neo-liberal policies in most states was to overlay a jury-rigged market economy on top of an inefficient command economy. At the same time, neo-liberalism shredded the "benefits for compliance" social pact that connected populations with their governments.

What was political life like in the Middle East up through 2010?

Every year, the Economist Intelligence Unit publishes a "Democracy Index."[2] The index ranks countries of the world according to such criteria as electoral process and pluralism, civil liberties, the functioning of government, political participation, and political culture. It then places each country in one of five categories that range from "full democracies" to "authoritarian regimes." How did the Middle East fare in 2010, the year in which the first of the Arab uprisings broke out?

Not well. In 2010 not one state in the Middle East made it into the category of "full democracy." Only one state—Israel— made it into the category of "flawed democracy," coming in at a ranking of #37 among all the countries of the world. In flawed democracies there are free and fair elections and respect for basic civil liberties. However, there are significant weaknesses in other democratic practices, including problems in governance. The next-highest-ranked state in the region was Lebanon (#86), followed by Turkey (#89), Palestine (#93), and Iraq (#111). *The Economist* called these states "hybrid democracies." Elections in all four had substantial irregularities and there were widespread corruption and weak nongovernmental institutions. (As of 2016, Lebanon's ranking had dropped to #102, Turkey's to #97, Palestine's to #110, and Iraq's to #114.)

All fifteen of the remaining countries in the Middle East fit into the category "authoritarian regimes." The lowest-ranked state was Saudi Arabia, which came in at #160 on a scale in which the lowest ranking overall was #167. On the whole, the Middle East had the lowest composite score of any region in the world, with the exception of sub-Saharan Africa.

From the different rankings on *The Economist* list, it is evident that the level of autocracy was not uniform across the region. Autocratic regimes came in various shapes and sizes. Although Kuwait (#114) and Jordan (#117), for example, are monarchies like Saudi Arabia, both have parliaments which can, at times, be defiant. Saudi Arabia does not. Nevertheless, in all three, kings maintain ultimate control: kings can dismiss prime ministers and appoint cabinets. Furthermore, in Kuwait and Jordan electoral districts are heavily gerrymandered.

Before its uprising, Egypt had a form of government that one political scientist called "semi-authoritarian."[3] In other words, the government allowed the opposition (the main component of which during the pre-uprising period was the Egyptian Muslim Brotherhood) some ability to organize and compete in elections, but no opportunity to win them. A United Nations report called Egypt, like most other Arab states, a "black hole state," meaning that the executive branch—that is, the office of president or king—was so powerful that it "converts the surrounding environment into a setting in which nothing moves and from which nothing escapes."[4]

Libya under its "brotherly leader" Muammar Qaddafi (who ruled from 1969 to 2011), on the other hand, claimed to have no government at all. Instead, it was a *jamahirriya*, a word made up by Qaddafi to mean "rule by the masses." Qaddafi maintained that Libya was a direct democracy in which everyone participated in governance without the mediation of representatives. Since such a system could not possibly work, Libya had, in fact, two governments: a "people's government" on paper and a real government, made up of Qaddafi, his kin, and those he favored, which actually ran the country. Libya narrowly beat out Saudi Arabia on *The Economist* index, tying Iran—an Islamic republic in which clerics, in alliance with the military, hold ultimate power—at #158.

Hybrid democracies differ in form as well as in ranking. For example, the Lebanese system might be termed a "sectarian oligarchy." Voters can choose their leaders from a list of the same old political bosses whose posts are determined by the religious sect to which they belong. In Turkey, hybrid democracy works until it doesn't. The culprit there has usually been the army, which assumed power in 1960, 1971, and 1980; forced the resignation of a prime minister in 1997; and tried (and failed) to take power again in 2016. Each time it assumed power, the army relinquished it only after "cleansing" the political system by disbanding parties and jailing (and frequently torturing) those it deemed enemies of the state. (Turkey is once again on an authoritarian path, but this time the guilty party—the president—dresses in civilian clothes.) On the other hand, the weakness, corruption, and incompetence of governance in Iraq and Palestine (which has had two competing governments since 2007) threaten the very integrity of each.

How did state formation in the region breed autocracies in the Middle East?

Autocratic structures were inscribed into the DNA of most states in the Middle East early on. The independent states that emerged in the region might be divided into three categories. First, there are those that emerged in the interwar period— Turkey, Iran, and Saudi Arabia. In all three, militaries played a key role in establishing the states, and military leaders became their initial rulers. Autocrats in Iran and Saudi Arabia both benefited from foreign (British) support and, in the case of the latter, the British offered protection to the future ruler before the state was founded. And it didn't hurt that autocratic models of state building and governance were readily available in a period during which Lenin, Hitler, and Mussolini took and held power.

The second category of state includes those that retained the structures the colonial powers had put in place or had sheltered after independence. Those powers had been interested in stability, not democracy. The states in this category include not only most of the remaining monarchies (Morocco, Jordan, Bahrain, Qatar, Kuwait, and the UAE), but Lebanon as well (Oman's relationship with Britain was more informal but significant nonetheless). The British and French viewed monarchs as reliable collaborators so long as they governed with a firm hand. As in Lebanon, the path to independence taken by monarchies was mainly peaceful (in the Gulf it was the British, not the various monarchs, who insisted that the statelets cut the cord). As a result, their transition from the colonial to the postcolonial era was marked more by continuity than rupture.

The final category of state consists of the postcolonial republics that took shape with the overthrow of the colonial order after independence: Tunisia (the only state in this category in which a civilian wrested control of the government, abolishing the monarchy), Algeria, Libya, Egypt, Syria, Iraq, and Yemen. Again, timing was everything: With the exception of Yemen—created through a shotgun wedding between two formerly independent Yemens in 1990—all emerged at the height of decolonization, when anti-imperialist revolutions and coups d'état undertaken by colonels hell-bent on destroying the remnants of the old order were the tactic du jour. Revolutionaries and coup plotters had little patience with democratic niceties. Their stated goals were typically to end the imperialist presence in their countries, to end feudalism (meaning, economic backwardness), and to end "corruption" (their term for the old boys' club of the former regime, which they sought to break up).

The Islamic Republic of Iran might also be placed in this category. Like Algeria, the Islamic republic was born of a mass uprising. And like all the others in this category, its leaders sought to root out most vestiges of the old regime.

How did great power meddling in the region foster autocracies in the Middle East?

In November 2003, President George W. Bush spoke before the National Endowment for Democracy and announced his "Freedom Agenda." "Sixty years of Western nations excusing and accommodating the lack of freedom in the Middle East did nothing to make us safe—because in the long run, stability cannot be purchased at the expense of liberty," he declared. "As long as the Middle East remains a place where freedom does not flourish, it will remain a place of stagnation, resentment, and violence ready for export."[5] He then announced what he called a "forward" strategy to advance freedom in the region.

Two years after he gave that speech, his secretary of state, Condoleezza Rice, paid a visit to Egypt to meet with Egyptian president Hosni Mubarak. She took the occasion to address students at the American University in Cairo. In her speech she reiterated Bush's remarks. "For sixty years, my country, the United States, pursued stability at the expense of democracy in this region here in the Middle East—and we achieved

neither. Now, we are taking a different course. We are supporting the democratic aspirations of all people."[6]

A year and a half later, however, Rice changed her tune. Instead
of pressuring Mubarak about human rights and democracy during a return visit to Cairo, she instead appealed for his help in
restarting stalled negotiations between Israelis and Palestinians.
The Bush administration's much vaunted, but fleeting, concern
for spreading American values had gone the way of other initia-
tives to put values ahead of immediate strategic need. American
policy reverted to its default position, which one political scientist has termed "democracy prevention."[7] Why haven't
American actions matched American rhetoric?

Over the course of the twentieth century, great powers—
meaning first Great Britain, then the United States—established
states, intervened directly into their internal affairs, or both.
They also protected those states from internal and external
threats. Great powers have used their leverage in both the political and economic spheres to dictate policy to governments
and have granted them financial assistance. Underwriting
democracy was not a high priority for those powers.

Great Britain was the predominant power in the region past
the end of World War II. That status was not to last. In the aftermath of the war, the United States, which had never before
had an equivalent stake in the region, took Britain's place as
the predominant power. In part this had to do with British
economic weakness and American economic strength. The
United States, fearing the spread of communism in the Gulf,
even offered to pay the insolvent British to remain there. In
part this had to do with the ability of the United States to insin-
uate itself into the conflict between Israel and the states that
surrounded it as an indispensable broker during the 1970s.
Egyptian president Anwar al-Sadat put it best. Appealing to
President Jimmy Carter to advance the Egyptian-Israeli peace
process, he declared that the United States "holds 99 percent of
the cards in the region in the Israel-Palestinian conflict."[8] And

in part this had to do with the role the United States played as leader of the "free world" during the Cold War.

American engagement with the region coincided with the onset of the Cold War, which defined US goals there. Throughout the Cold War, the United States sought to attain six goals in the region: prevent the expansion of Soviet influence; ensure Western access to oil; secure the peaceful resolution of conflicts and foster a regional balance of power; promote stable, pro-Western states in the region; preserve the independence and territorial integrity of the state of Israel; and protect the sea lanes, lines of communications, civil aviation routes, and the like connecting the United States and Europe with Asia.

Autocratic regimes were useful in achieving all these goals. For example, American policy makers believed that only strong, autocratic regimes could bring about the rapid economic development necessary to prevent their populations from "going communist." Only strong, autocratic regimes such as that in Egypt, they believed, could sign peace treaties with Israel in the face of popular opposition to those treaties. And, they believed, only strong, autocratic regimes that maintained a regional balance of power could ensure the uninterrupted supply of oil to the United States and its allies.

American support for autocrats was both direct and indirect. The United States directly and indirectly supported military officers who seized power in states throughout the region from the late 1940s through the 1960s. For example, the United States backed (some say sponsored) the first post-independence coup d'état in Syria—the first coup in the Arab world following World War II. The coup overthrew a democratically elected government. And, of course, the United States directly and indirectly supported a host of autocratic kings and emirs. This began even before the end of World War II, when Saudi Arabia became the only neutral state to receive American Lend-Lease assistance.

When the Cold War ended, the United States maintained five of its six policy goals in the region (containing the Soviet Union, which was dismantled in 1991, was, of course, no longer necessary). As a result, the United States continued to support autocratic regimes. For example, the United States headed the coalition that threw Iraq out of Kuwait in 1991. It thus maintained the Middle East state system and balance of power as it had been before the invasion. It also assured the uninterrupted flow of oil. The United States then turned its back on Kuwaiti pro-democracy groups agitating for truly representative institutions in the kingdom.

After 9/11, the United States added another policy goal: It declared the Global War on Terrorism (GWOT), which proved a boon to friend and foe alike. Autocrats such as Hosni Mubarak of Egypt, Ali Abdullah Saleh of Yemen, and even Muammar Qaddafi of Libya and Bashar al-Assad of Syria managed to put themselves on the side of angels. Mubarak and Assad accepted and interrogated suspected terrorists using torture, Saleh allowed the United States to fight its war on terror on his country's soil, and Qaddafi renounced his weapons of mass destruction. Interestingly, GWOT, which George W. Bush announced even before the Freedom Agenda, was one of the reasons the former president abandoned America's fleeting interest in promoting democracy.

How has the exploitation of oil affected the Middle East?

Ever since the British Royal Navy switched from coal to oil to fuel its ships in the early twentieth century, Middle Eastern oil has loomed large in the strategic calculus of great powers. Hence, the United States and Britain organized a coup d'état that overthrew the democratically elected prime minister of Iran in 1953. His crime? He nationalized the British-owned oil company that operated in his country. Hence, the Fifth Fleet patrols the waters of the Persian Gulf. And hence, ongoing American support for some of the most hideous regimes on the planet that keep the oil flowing. Myanmar got sanctions; Saudi Arabia got F-15 Eagles.

Although oil began to flow from the Arabian Peninsula in 1938, Middle Easterners themselves did not begin to feel the revolutionary effects of oil production until the 1970s. That was when the oil-producing states in the region and elsewhere launched successful campaigns to wrest control of the pricing, production quotas, and ownership of their oil from the foreign-owned oil companies that had dominated the business until then. As a result of these campaigns, an unprecedented amount of wealth flowed into the Middle East.

What became known as the "oil price revolution"—the 380 percent increase in the price of oil during four months in 1973–74—transformed the Arabian Peninsula from a cultural and political backwater into a regional powerhouse. Within ten years, oil exporters—the wealthiest of which were concentrated in the region at the time—had accumulated $1.7 trillion. The Gulf exporters in particular used this money to win friends and influence people. From 1973 to 1978, for example, Egypt alone received $17 billion from Arab oil producers in the form of grants and loans. Between 1973 and 1983, assistance from abroad paid for *all* of Yemen's government spending. With small populations and weak militaries, Gulf states were thus able to punch above their diplomatic weight. It is no coincidence that the peace accord that ended the fifteen-year Lebanese civil war in 1989 is called the Taif Agreement, after the city in Saudi Arabia where it was negotiated.

Oil producers maintained leverage over their neighbors through labor policies as well. Because of their small size, the newly enriched oil producers had to rely on guest workers to keep their recharged economies humming and to build infrastructure. Initially, those guest workers came from the Arab world. In 1968, for example, no more than 10,000 Egyptians worked abroad. Within ten years, that number had increased to over half a million. A decade later, another million Egyptian workers found employment in Iraq. Sending their excess labor abroad benefited the states in the region that were not blessed with oil. It enabled them to sidestep the disquieting consequences of high unemployment. In addition, the money those workers sent home to their families reduced the burden of providing welfare and services for cash-strapped governments. Importing labor provided oil-rich states with an opportunity to coerce or punish their neighbors. Thus, when Egypt joined the Gulf War coalition, Iraq expelled its resident Egyptians.

Although Arabs initially made up a vast majority of guest workers in the Gulf, the Gulf states feared those workers might bring with them politically and socially subversive ideas which, as Arabic speakers, they might spread to native populations. As a result, Gulf states increasingly looked to their own populations for labor—a policy called "job nationalization." They also looked to South Asia. In 1975, 90 percent of the foreign workers in the Gulf came from Arab countries; twenty years later, that number had dropped to 38 percent. This, of course, closed the social safety valve upon which non-oil producers had come to rely.

The oil price revolution had two other effects on the region. First, it made the entire region—not just the oil producers—overly dependent on global markets. When the price of oil goes down, so do national incomes. And even though most oil-rich states have placed a sizable chunk of their earnings in sovereign wealth funds (state-owned investment funds) just in case, cashing in even a modest amount of those funds would depress the markets in which they are invested, thus lowering their value.

In addition, direct and indirect rent income from oil has contributed to the number and durability of autocracies in the region. Throughout the Arab world, states do not have to go to their populations, hat in hand, soliciting money. And oil revenue has provided states the wherewithal to subsidize welfare and services for their citizens, manipulate public attitudes and behaviors, and fight external aggression and domestic insurrection. As events since 2010 demonstrate, the use of money derived from oil for these purposes has not been foolproof. But it is not to be discounted, either.

What is the "New Middle East"?

If credit is to be given to anyone for coining the phrase "New Middle East," that credit should go to Condoleezza Rice. In 2006, Israel invaded Lebanon. The invasion came in response to a cross-border raid and rocket attacks launched at Israel from Lebanon by Hizbullah, a Lebanese group that is a combination of militia, political party, and service provider. Nevertheless, the damage inflicted by the Israeli army on Lebanon was appalling, even by Middle East standards: Between 800 and 1,200 Lebanese died, many of them civilians (UNICEF estimated that upward of one third of the victims were children under the age of thirteen). Estimates of the damage to Lebanese infrastructure hovered around $2.5 billion.

In the midst of the carnage, Rice held a press conference at which she declared that what the world was witnessing in Lebanon was the "birth pangs of a new Middle East."[9] What Rice meant was that slapping down groups like Hizbullah would clear the way for the emergence of a more peaceful and democratic region. While Hizbullah was hardly slapped down, she was, in a way, correct: The war did herald the emergence of a new Middle East—one that was significantly more violent and unpredictable than its predecessor.

About a year and a half after Rice's comment, an American diplomat and policy analyst, Richard N. Haass, wrote an article for the journal *Foreign Affairs,* titled "The New Middle East."[10] According to Haass, the era of the "old" Middle East, defined in large measure by *pax Americana* ("American peace"), had drawn to a close. It had ended as a result of the American invasion of Iraq, the collapse of the Israeli-Palestinian peace process, the failure of Arab regimes to deal with radical Islam, and globalization. He then outlined twelve distinctive features of the era that was just beginning. While recounting them all is unnecessary here, suffice it to say that given the unforeseeable events of the 2010s, most of Haass's predictions were remarkably prescient.

In the chapters that follow, this book explores the contours of the New Middle East. Although it might be argued that the impact of twenty-first century events on the region pales in comparison to the impact of, for example, nineteenth-century imperialism or World War I, it cannot be denied that the impact is, nevertheless, significant. Indeed, it is entirely possible that those events will leave a permanent mark on the politics, economics, society, and even demography of the region.

Three events gave rise to the New Middle East. The first was the collapse of the Soviet Union in 1991. That collapse marked the demise of the overarching American strategy in the region, along with the unity of purpose that joined the United States with its partners there. The American invasion of Iraq, which would not have occurred during the Cold War lest the United States take its eyes off the prize of containing the Soviet Union, was, in large measure, a symptom of a superpower's floundering to find a new strategy, if not purpose, in the region.

The second and third events not only set the stage for the New Middle East, they played a key role in shaping it. Those events were the American invasion and occupation of Iraq, which began in 2003, and the Arab uprisings, which began in December 2010 (but whose roots stretch back much further).

Although the American invasion of Iraq resulted in the overthrow of the regime that had ruled over that long-suffering country, it brought chaos in its wake. It also brought a post-occupation government that neither ruled effectively nor won the support of much of the Iraqi population. Likewise, the giddiness that accompanied the early days of the Arab uprisings all too quickly soured in the prisons of Egypt and Bahrain and on the killing fields of Syria, Libya, and Yemen. Both events upset the regional order and unleashed mayhem—from state breakdown, inter-sectarian conflict, and the rise of the Islamic State in Iraq and Syria (ISIS), to proxy wars, humanitarian crises, and appalling displays of brutality—that had either been held in check or had not existed before.

2

THE ARAB UPRISINGS AND THEIR FALLOUT

How did the Arab uprisings begin?

On December 17, 2010, a Tunisian street vendor, Muhammad Bouazizi, set himself on fire in front of the local government building in Sidi Bouzid, a town in central Tunisia. Earlier in the day, a policewoman had confiscated his wares and publicly humiliated him. He tried to complain at the local municipality, but to no avail. It was then that he went to the local market and bought the flammable liquid with which he doused himself.

Bouazizi's act struck a chord among Tunisians, and protests quickly spread from Sidi Bouzid across the country. Tunisian protesters brought a number of issues to the table: unemployment, food inflation, corruption, poor living conditions, lack of freedoms, and lack of government responsiveness. The Tunisian General Labor Union (UGTT), the sometime lapdog of the regime, saw which way the wind was blowing and threw its support behind the protests. The UGTT had more than 600,000 members.

At first, Tunisian president Zine al-Abidine bin Ali, who had ruled for a quarter of a century, tried to pacify the protesters. In a pattern that was repeated time after time in the Arab world, he promised 300,000 new jobs, new parliamentary elections, and a "national dialogue." This did little to mollify them. On January 14, 2011—less than a month after Bouazizi's self-immolation—military and political leaders decided enough was enough. With the army surrounding the presidential palace, bin Ali resigned and appointed his prime minister to head a caretaker government. Continued protests forced the appointment of another prime minister, not as closely identified with the old regime. The uprising in Tunisia was the first ever in the modern Arab world to bring down an autocrat.

About a week and a half after bin Ali resigned, young people, many of whom belonged to the "April 6 Youth Movement," began their occupation of Tahrir Square in Cairo. (While Tahrir Square was but one site of many in Egypt where protests were held that day, it emerged as the symbolic center of the Egyptian uprising.) The April 6 Youth Movement got its name from a date in 2008 when young people, using Facebook, called for a general strike to support striking workers at a state-run textile factory. The general strike failed, giving lie to the miraculous powers frequently ascribed to Facebook and other social media by breathless Western commentators.

That was 2008. This time around, protesters were more successful. The security forces and goons-for-hire failed to dislodge them from the square. Then the army announced it would not fire on them. Strikes and anti-government protests spread throughout Egypt. On February 11, 2011, the army took matters into its own hands. It deposed President Hosni Mubarak and established a new government under the Supreme Council of the Armed Forces. This phase of the Egyptian uprising—what might be called the first street phase of the Egyptian uprising—was over in a mere eighteen days.

Soon after the Tunisian and Egyptian uprisings seemingly demonstrated what could be done, populations elsewhere began to smell blood in the water and followed suit. In spite of the obvious influence the first two uprisings had on those that followed, however, it would be wrong to view them through the lens of the first two. For example, after the outbreak of the Egyptian uprising, a similar protest movement emerged in Yemen. Nevertheless, it had very un-Tunisian, un-Egyptian results. As supporters of the regime squared off against social-networking youths and labor, along with military officers, disgruntled tribesmen, and opposition members of parliament whom the regime had failed to buy off, Yemen descended into chaos and violence. Ever since, Yemen has suffered through extended periods of bloodshed intermittently interrupted by outside attempts to broker national reconciliation.

Uprisings in both Libya and Syria also turned into long, violent affairs. In Libya, dissidents called for a "Day of Rage" after the arrest of a prominent human-rights lawyer. He represented families of the 1,200 "disappeared" political prisoners who had been murdered in cold blood in one single incident in 1996. A six-month civil war followed, which ended only after a fierce NATO air campaign targeted the regime. And after months of predictions that "it couldn't happen in Syria," it did. As in Libya, a spontaneous uprising in a town far from the capital sparked a seemingly endless and bloody antigovernment insurrection. However the Syrian uprising ends, neither the Syrian people nor the villages and cities in which they live will ever return to their pre-uprising condition.

Protesters challenged monarchies as well. After protests modeled on those of Egypt broke out in Bahrain, the government struck back violently. Using the excuse that Iranian subversion was behind the protests, it invited in troops and police from neighboring Saudi Arabia and the UAE to help "restore order." A period of brutal repression followed. As in Libya, outside intervention determined the course of an uprising. In Saudi Arabia and Morocco, kings who had presented themselves as "reformers" faced protesters who demanded expanded representation, an end to corruption, and constitutional checks on monarchic power. Significantly, protesters did not demand the replacement of the regime, as protesters elsewhere had done. Both governments sought to calm the waters by offering their citizens inducements. The Saudi government promised a $130 billion benefits package for its citizens. The Moroccan government agreed to superficial reforms.

These were the main sites of contention during the four months of what has been dubbed the "Arab Spring." There were other sites as well. There were also sites where populations took to the streets after the initial wave had crested. All told, since Bouazizi's suicide, protests or uprisings have broken out in at least eighteen of the twenty-two states that consider themselves part of the Arab world.

How appropriate is the term "Arab Spring" to describe the uprisings?

There are two terms commonly used to describe what has happened in the Arab world since December 2010. The first and most popular is "Arab Spring." This term might have seemed appropriate in the early, heady days of the uprisings. Today, however, it appears more ironic than descriptive. There are other problems with the term as well. For one, the uprisings were not entirely Arab. In Libya, for example, Berbers played an important role in toppling the regime. Nor can events in the Arab world during 2010–11 be viewed as a discrete phenomenon that might be isolated within the span of a single "season." Not only did some uprisings continue in one form or another afterward, others began long after the arrival of the 2011 summer solstice. Furthermore, the so-called Arab Spring was not a unique event in Arab history; rather, it was but the latest phase in a three-decade-long struggle for human and democratic rights and social and economic justice in the region.

The second term commonly used to describe what has been happening in the Arab world since Bouazizi's death is "wave," as in a "revolutionary wave." There are pluses and minuses to viewing the uprisings as a wave. On the plus side, there is no denying that later Arab uprisings borrowed techniques of mobilization and symbols from earlier ones. Town squares that became the sites of protest throughout the Arab world were renamed "Tahrir," after the main site of protest in Cairo, and many uprisings began with a scheduled "Day of Rage," also borrowed from the Egyptian model. Then there is the highly touted use of social-networking sites for the purpose of mobilization, not to mention the common demands for human and democratic rights and social justice.

There are, however, two main objections to the use of the wave metaphor. Most significantly, the metaphor makes it seem that the spread of the uprisings and protests from state to state was inevitable, like a wave washing over a beach. Its use thus obscures the fact that the uprisings and protests spread as a result of tens of thousands of individual decisions made by participants who chose on a daily basis to face the full repressive power of their governments. The wave metaphor also obscures the fact that the goals and styles of the uprisings and protests have varied widely from country to country. The goal of some has been the complete overthrow of the regime, while the goal of others has been the reform of the regime. In some places, initial protests came about after meticulous preparation; in others, the spark was spontaneous. And there have been times when uprisings have been predominantly peaceful and other times when they took a violent turn.

Despite the metaphor's problems, thinking of the Arab uprisings in terms of a wave is useful if it is understood that what happened in the Arab world in 2010–11 not only had a region-wide dimension, but a local one as well. There were, of course, a number of factors that made it likely that an uprising in one or another place would find a sympathetic audience elsewhere in the region. Since the 1950s, for example, all Arab states came to share similar characteristics. And since the mid-1970s, all Arab states have faced similar conditions and shocks that have made them vulnerable to popular anger. Nevertheless, variations in local history, state structure, and state capability shaped the course of each uprising. Those variations made it impossible for Libyans, Yemenis, or Syrians, for example, to replicate the relative peacefulness and quick resolution which marked the initial phases of the Tunisian and Egyptian uprisings.

And there was an additional factor that shaped the path of a number of the uprisings: foreign intervention. States both outside and within the region had an interest in the outcomes of the various uprisings and acted accordingly. Some wanted one or another uprising to succeed, others, to fail. Indeed, in Libya, Yemen, Bahrain, Syria, and even Egypt, foreign assistance proved decisive for successes enjoyed by insurgents (Libya), counterinsurgents (Yemen, Bahrain, Egypt), or both (Syria).

What deep-seated factors made Arab states vulnerable to popular anger?

Overall, there are five region-wide factors that made all states in the Arab world vulnerable to popular anger. Three of these were deep seated; two were contingent (that is, fortuitous and unpredictable). None of these factors actually *caused* the uprisings, per se. To attribute causation to these or any other factors overlooks a key variable—the human element—that determines whether an uprising will or will not occur. That Tunisians would connect a tragic death to the corruption and brutality of the regime that governed them, and then risk their lives to remove that regime, was not inevitable. People making choices in real time drove the uprisings.

The first long-term factor that made Arab states vulnerable to popular anger was neo-liberalism. When states adopted neo-liberal policies, they effectively tore up the "benefits for compliance" ruling bargain that had bound populations to their governments.

Neo-liberalism got its tentative start in the Arab world in December 1976, when Egypt negotiated a $450 million credit line with the IMF. In return, the Egyptian government pledged to cut commodity supports and direct subsidies. Over the next three decades, the IMF negotiated ever more expansive agreements with cash-strapped governments throughout the region. But by obeying the dictates of the IMF, governments encountered resistance from their populations, who engaged in acts of defiance that ranged from revolt (so-called IMF riots) to labor activism.

Populations found two aspects of neo-liberalism particularly repellent. The first was the fraying of the social safety net and threats to middle-class welfare. Of particular concern were threats to across-the-board subsidies for food and fuel. At the recommendation of the IMF, those subsidies were replaced by subsidies targeted to those who lived in "extreme poverty." Populations also took a dim view of the sell-off of publicly owned enterprises to private entrepreneurs—a policy known as privatization. For many, privatization threatened state-employment guarantees. Furthermore, privatization did not lead, as its proponents promised, to free-market capitalism, but rather to crony capitalism, as regime loyalists took advantage of their access to the corridors of power. Privatization also widened the gulf between rich and poor. The worst of the crony capitalists thus came to symbolize systemic corruption in the buildup to the uprisings, and select crony capitalists heard their names chanted on the streets during them.

Accompanying the neo-liberal revolution was the so-called Human Rights Revolution, which began in the mid-1970s— the second factor that made states in the region vulnerable. The term "Human Rights Revolution" refers to two phenomena. First, it refers to a transformation of the notion of human rights. Before the 1970s, the words "human rights" referred to a breadbasket of rights: collective rights (such as the right of a nation to self-determination), economic rights (such as a person's right to a job), and individual rights (freedom of assembly, freedom from torture). After the revolution, the last meaning became predominant, particularly when used in international law. In addition, the term "Human Rights Revolution" refers to a time when governments (particularly in the West) and nongovernmental organizations alike put the rights of citizens on the international agenda.

It is no coincidence that the advance of neo-liberalism and the Human Rights Revolution took place simultaneously. Both privileged the rights of individuals over the rights of states or groups. Neo-liberalism did so in terms of individuals' economic rights; the Human Rights Revolution in terms of their political, civil, and personal rights. In theory, the two are interconnected. A free market depends on autonomous, rights-bearing individuals who need to be free to gather information, make decisions, and enter into voluntary associations with one another, whether on the floor of a stock exchange or in a town hall meeting. The United States found it useful to conjoin the two in its diplomatic endeavors. Together, they provided a comprehensive alternative to the collectivism and state-centrism of the Soviet Union and the newly assertive independent states of the postcolonial world.

The Arab world was not impervious to the Human Rights Revolution. A wide variety of individuals, from leftists and liberals to members of the loyal opposition and even Muslim clerics, found human rights to be an effective tool in the struggle against their autocratic governments. It was no accident, then, that the uprisings of 2010–11 initially spoke in the language of human rights, as well as democratic rights, no matter how they evolved over time.

The third long-term factor that made Arab regimes vulnerable was their brittleness. The years between the onset of the economic crisis of 2008 and the Tunisian uprising were not good ones for governments throughout the world. Governments found themselves caught between bankers and economists recommending austerity, on the one hand, and populations fearing the end of the welfare state that provided for them, on the other. While uprisings were spreading in the Arab world, governments fell in the United Kingdom, Greece, Ireland, Portugal, Spain, Iceland, Italy, and elsewhere, and were challenged in France and the United States. Throughout it all, not one government was overthrown, nor were political institutions uprooted. Blame fell on politicians and parties and the policies they pushed.

In the Arab world, populations could not turn popular representatives out of office because there were no popular representatives. This is why populations throughout the region took to the streets as their first option. This also explains why the most common slogan during this period was "The people demand the downfall of the *nizam* [regime]," not "The people demand the downfall of the *hukuma* [government]."

What contingent factors made Arab states vulnerable to popular anger?

In addition to the deep-seated factors that made Arab states vulnerable to popular anger, there were two contingent ones. The first of these was demography. In 2011, approximately 60 percent of the population of the Arab world was under the age of thirty. Even more telling was the percentage of youth between the ages of fifteen and twenty-nine, the period during which most enter the job market and compete on the marriage market. In 2010, youths between the ages of fifteen and twenty-nine made up 29 percent of the population of Tunisia, 30 percent of the population of Egypt, and 34 percent of the population of Libya. They also made up the bulk of the unemployed (in Egypt they made up 90 percent of the unemployed).

Demography is not, of course, destiny, and frustrations about job or life prospects do not necessarily translate into rebellion. Furthermore, youth was hardly the only segment of the Arab population that mobilized during the uprisings: In Tunisia and Egypt, labor played a major role; in Libya and Syria, parents protesting the way the state had dealt with their children sparked them. Nevertheless, by 2010 there was a cohort of youths throughout the Arab world with a significant set of grievances. Under the proper circumstances, this cohort was available to be mobilized for oppositional politics.

The other contingent factor that made regimes in the Arab world vulnerable was a global rise in food prices. Between mid-2010 and January 2011, the world price of wheat, for example, more than doubled. Economists attribute this price rise to a number of factors, from speculation to drought to more acreage in the United States and Europe devoted to growing corn for biofuel.

The Arab Middle East is more dependent on imported food than is any other region in the world. At the time of its uprising, Egypt was the world's largest wheat importer. In addition to its dependence on food imports, however, there are two other reasons that skyrocketing food prices are a particular burden in the Arab world. First, the portion of household spending that goes to pay for food in the Arab world ranges as high as 63 percent in Morocco. Compare that to the average percentage of household spending that goes to pay for food in the United States: 7 percent—a figure that includes eating as entertainment (that is, dining outside the home). The second reason skyrocketing food prices in the Arab world were particularly punishing is neo-liberalism. Pressure from the United States and the IMF has constrained governments from intervening into markets to fix prices and has forced governments to abandon across-the-board subsidies on food.

What were the uprisings like in Tunisia and Egypt?

Once uprisings and protests began to break out in the region, they took a number of forms. In the main, the ones that have broken out thus far might be placed into five clusters: Tunisia and Egypt; Yemen and Libya; Bahrain and Syria; the monarchies; and Iraq, Lebanon, and Palestine.

Let us start with Tunisia and Egypt. During the uprisings in the two states, militaries stepped in to depose long-ruling autocrats who faced widespread disaffection. The militaries thus cut the revolutionary process short. This prevented a thorough house-cleaning in both places.

Tunisia and Egypt are unique in the Arab world. Beginning in the nineteenth century, both experienced two centuries of continuous state-building. As a result, in both there were long-lived, functioning institutions autonomous from (although subservient to) the executive branch of the government. The military was one of those institutions, but there were others as well, including the judiciary and security services. Together, these institutions make up what political scientists call the "deep state." When faced with an unprecedented crisis, the institutions of the deep state closed ranks to protect the old order.

The struggle between the deep state and the forces promoting change in Tunisia and Egypt defined the course of the two uprisings. When moderate Islamist organizations—Ennahda in Tunisia, the Muslim Brotherhood in Egypt—won popular mandates to form governments at the conclusion of the initial phase of the uprisings, the deep state joined forces with remnants of the old regime and more secular-oriented groups within the population in defiance. In Egypt, the brotherhood saw itself locked in a battle to the death with its adversaries, which felt likewise. It therefore refused to share power with them, and even pushed through a constitution it drafted when it appeared that the judiciary was about to dissolve the constitutional assembly on procedural grounds. As the crisis escalated—and as the Egyptian economy went into a free fall—hundreds of thousands of Egyptians once again took to the streets. And, once again, the military stepped in. It dissolved the brotherhood, had a new constitution drafted which enhanced the power of the deep state, and established a regime far more repressive than Mubarak's. According to the Egyptian Centre for Economic and Social Rights, during the first four months following its takeover, the military killed 2,665 of their fellow citizens, wounded 16,000, and arrested 13,145.[1]

Events in Tunisia did not end up as badly. Unlike the Egyptian Muslim Brotherhood, Ennahda did not overplay its hand. From the beginning, in fact, Ennahda reached out to opposition parties and brought them into the government. And when faced with the same crises and oppositional forces faced by the Egyptian Muslim Brotherhood, Ennahda, as well as its opponents, stepped away from the precipice. Ennahda dissolved the government it dominated and called for new elections (which it lost). It also agreed to the most liberal constitution in the Arab world. That constitution does not refer to Islamic law at all and it promises women the same number of seats as men in all elected bodies. Although the economic and political stability of Tunisia continues to be threatened by violence from militant groups like ISIS, if any of the uprisings is to have a happy ending the Tunisian uprising is the most likely candidate.

What did almost everyone get wrong about the Egyptian Revolution?

In the popular imagination, the Egyptian uprising conjures up a number of associations: tech-savvy youths who played the starring role in bringing down Hosni Mubarak; nonviolent resistance, similar to that employed by the people-power uprisings of the 1980s in Indonesia, the Philippines, South Korea, Taiwan, and elsewhere; appeals lodged by protesters for their long-overdue civil and political rights; the standing down of the "people's army" and the supreme command's decision to defuse the crisis by removing Mubarak itself; and a victorious popular movement that overthrew an entrenched autocrat in eighteen days.

These associations are powerful—but inaccurate. Here's what they get wrong:

- The idea that tech-savvy youths brought down Mubarak is wrong on two counts. First, data collected after the fact indicate that 59 percent of Egyptian protesters were between the ages of twenty-five and forty-four—a rather expansive definition of "youth." Second, in Egypt (as in Tunisia and Yemen) labor played a critical role—perhaps *the* critical role—in the uprising. It is probably no coincidence that the army forced Mubarak to step down only days after a strike wave brought the Egyptian economy—of which the military is the largest stakeholder—to a standstill.

- The uprising was hardly peaceful, either, as the so-called Battle of the Camel—the televised attack on Tahrir Square protesters by hooligans mounted on donkeys and camels—confirms. That the protesters held their ground had less to do with what Obama called "the moral force of nonviolence"[2] than it did with street-fighting "ultras"—football thugs—who rumbled with the hired goons, shielding those within the square.

- Away from the cameras—in the city of Suez and elsewhere—protests were violent from the start. Throughout Egypt, arsonists torched hundreds of police stations and buildings housing offices of the ruling National Democratic Party. Overall, the newspaper *al-Masry al-Youm/Egypt Independent* tallied about 850 fatalities and 6,000 injuries during those eighteen days.[3]

- In contrast to the slogan, "The army and the people are one," an official government report later charged the army with disappearing about 1,200 Egyptians—many permanently—in the lead-up to February 11. More were to follow.

- According to polling data, nearly twice as many protesters cited the economy as a principal factor in their participation as cited their quest for civil and political rights. The ratio was even higher among protesters who supported the July 3, 2013 military coup against the popularly elected Muslim Brotherhood president.

- The removal of Mubarak did little to transform the institutions and structures of the deep state. In fact, Egypt's new constitution enshrines their power and autonomy.

Why have Islamic movements been so popular in the Middle East?

The terms "Islamism" and "Islamic movements" embrace a grab bag of associations, parties, and governments that seek to order their societies according to what they consider to be Islamic principles. The term "Islamist" refers to those who profess those principles. Some Islamists choose to participate in politics to achieve this end; others do not. Some use violence to achieve their goals; others have participated in the political process. Some believe that Islamic principles provide them with a strict roadmap to be followed without deviation; others treat those principles more gingerly. Hence, the attempt by some Islamists to meld human rights and democracy with Islamic principles.

Islamist parties won the first free elections in Tunisia and Egypt. They have done well elsewhere, such as in Yemen, Morocco, Algeria, Palestine, and Jordan. This begs the question: "Why?"

It is commonplace to treat Islamist movements as a special category of political movement. This is because the goals of Islamist movements—establishing regimes that observe and enforce Islamic law, for example—differ from the goals of other political movements. But rather than focusing on the distinctive goals of Islamist movements, we might do better to understand them within a comparative framework. This would make Islamist movements (and those who follow them) appear less idiosyncratic and explain their appeal.

In the main, there have been four possible foundations for social and political movements in the modern Middle East, as elsewhere in the contemporary world: utopianism, demands for the restoration or expansion of rights, nativism, or some combination thereof. The category of utopianism includes Marxist and anarchist movements—movements that seek to create a world that does not yet exist. While most Marxists and anarchists have a roadmap for what they seek to accomplish (*Das Kapital*, for example), they do not have much nostalgia for the past. Conversely, those who make demands for rights—be they for social and economic justice or for collective or individual rights—do not want to abolish the current order; they want to reform it or join it on an equal footing. All the uprisings that took place in the Arab world in 2010–11 made claims for rights.

Then there are nativist movements. Nativists believe that the only means to bring about the regeneration of a particular community is for that community to embrace its authentic, defining traditions. Like movements based on the demand for rights, nativist movements are commonplace in the modern world. For example, nativism provides the ideological foundation for the Hindu nationalist party in India, the Bharatiya Janata Party, as well as for the slogan "Make America great again." And they are popular, as can be seen from their current resurgence worldwide. The only thing that makes nativism in the Islamic world different from nativism elsewhere is that Islam can be mobilized to play a role in defining authenticity there.

Some social and political movements have been exclusively nativist or rights-based. Wahhabism (the official ideology of Saudi Arabia) is exclusively nativist. Its followers advocate returning to the Islam they believe Muhammad and the first Islamic community practiced.

Wahhabism is a form of salafism. Salafism refers to a technique some Muslims use for discovering religious truth. Salafis believe they can rely on only two sources to get at that truth: the Qur'an (which, for Muslims, is an emanation from God), and the sayings and acts of the prophet Muhammad and his seventh-century companions. As a result, all salafis are nativists, whether they choose to participate in politics (like ISIS and the Taliban in Afghanistan), or not.

On the other hand, contemporary labor activism and consumer boycotts usually speak the language of economic justice without appeals to tradition. So did the IMF riots that spread throughout the region in the 1980s.

Most modern social and political movements, however, have combined nativism with an appeal to rights. The few remaining stateless nationalities in the region—the Palestinians, the Kurds, the Sahrawis in southern Morocco—certainly do. So do all nationalists, who claim a right to self-determination based on a distinct linguistic, ethnic, religious, or historical tradition. Likewise, other groups. For example, in 1980 the Berber community of Algeria mounted protests demanding the government in Algiers recognize their collective right to maintain their Berber identity and their language, Tamazight. In other words, the so-called Berber Spring claimed the right for Algerian Berbers to maintain their traditions. And the various Islamists and Islamist groups that, at various times, embraced the platform of human rights, democratic participation, or both—including the Muslim Brotherhood of Egypt and Ennahda—have combined nativism with a demand for rights as well.

Why were uprisings in Yemen and Libya so violent?

In both Yemen and Libya, regimes fragmented, pitting the officers and soldiers, cabinet ministers, politicians, and diplomats who stood with the regime against those who joined the opposition.

The fragmentation of regimes in the two states is not surprising: In contrast to Tunisia and Egypt, both Yemen and Libya are poster children for what political scientists call "weak states." In weak states, governments and the bureaucracies upon which they depend are unable to assert their authority over the entirety of the territory they rule. Nor are they able to extend their reach beneath the surface of society. It is partly for this reason that populations in weak states lack strong national identities and allegiances. Such is the situation in both Yemen and Libya.

To a certain extent, the weakness of the Yemeni and Libyan states came about as a result of geography. Neither country has terrain that makes it easy to govern—Yemen because of the roughness of its terrain, Libya because of the terrain's expansiveness. To a certain extent, the weakness of the Yemeni and Libyan states is a result of their history (or lack thereof). Both states are relatively recent creations that combine disparate territories and populations. Yemen had been divided between an independent North Yemen and South Yemen until 1990. Contrasting social structures found in each Yemen reflect the legacies of formal imperialism in the south and the absence of formal imperialism in the north. The United Nations created an independent federated Libya in 1952 from the remnants of three former Italian colonies which had been kept separate until 1934. Even then, regional differences remained.

The final reason for the weakness of the Yemeni and Libyan states was the ruling styles of their leaders. Both President Ali Abdullah Saleh of Yemen, who ruled Yemen since its founding in 1990, and Muammar Qaddafi of Libya, who took power in 1969, purposely avoided establishing strong institutions. Instead, they favored a personalistic style of rule. This gave them more leeway in playing off tribes and other internal groupings against one another.

Because regimes in both states fragmented, there was no unified military to step in to end the uprisings, as had happened in Tunisia and Egypt. As a result, uprisings in both states were both violent and long and invited foreign meddling. In the case of Yemen, the Gulf Cooperation Council (or GCC—an economic, political, and military association made up of Gulf monarchies, along with Saudi Arabia, which dominates it), the United States, and the United Nations intervened to foster a "national dialogue." Since the outside world was more interested in stability than democratic transition, the dialogue mainly included the pre-uprising political elites. Their greatest interest was in claiming their share of the pie.

In the end, foreign powers got neither democratic transition nor stability. A Southern secessionist movement, which did not participate in the national dialogue, reasserted itself in Yemen. So did the Houthi movement, named after a leading family within

Yemen's Zaydi religious minority, which makes up roughly 40 percent of the Yemeni population. The Houthis joined forces with Ali Abdullah Saleh to take control of the capital and depose the first post-uprising government. Opposed to the Houthi/Saleh alliance was an international coalition led by Saudi Arabia, which intervened by air and sea to restore the deposed government. Years after the initial uprising, Yemen, a country that had always been on the brink, became a humanitarian nightmare.

As for Libya, locally based militias—some Islamist, some not—vied for control over resources, territory, and political power in the immediate aftermath of the uprising. Over time, Islamist militias, on the one hand, and non-Islamist militias and regime holdovers, on the other, coalesced into two opposing camps represented by two different governments. And, over time, the battlefield became even more complex, as forces under the command of a UN-brokered Government of National Accord and ISIS joined the fray.

As in Tunisia and Egypt, then, the main fault line in Libyan politics in the aftermath of the February 2011 uprising became one separating Islamists from their anti-Islamist opponents. Unlike the case of Tunisia, however, outside powers have fueled the Libyan flames. First, there was NATO. Then Qatar supplied Islamists with weaponry while Egypt and the UAE spearheaded military intervention on behalf of their secular opponents. Finally, as ISIS consolidated its position there, Libya became another front in the American-led war on terrorism in general and its war on ISIS in particular.

How could regimes in Bahrain and Syria hold on so doggedly?

Unlike Tunisia and Egypt, where one faction in the ruling elite turned on another, and unlike Yemen and Libya, where regimes splintered as a result of the shock of the uprisings there, regimes in Syria and Bahrain maintained their cohesion against the uprisings. One might even say that in Syria and Bahrain regimes had no choice but to maintain their cohesion against uprisings: Rulers of both states effectively "coup-proofed"[4] their regimes by, among other things, exploiting ties of sect and kinship to build a close-knit, interdependent ruling group.

The ruling group in Syria consists of President Bashar al-Assad, his extended family, and members of the minority Alawite community (which makes up anywhere from 12 to 17 percent of the Syrian population, depending on whom you ask). When the uprising began, President Bashar al-Assad's cousin was the head of the presidential guard, his brother was commander of the Republican Guard and Fourth Armored Division, and his now deceased brother-in-law was deputy chief of staff. None of them could have turned on the regime. If the regime went, they would go, too. As a matter of fact, few persons of note have defected from the regime and, of those who have—one brigadier general, a prime minister (which in Syria is a post of little importance), and an ambassador to Iraq—not one was Alawite.

The core of the regime in Bahrain consists of members of the ruling Khalifa family, who hold critical cabinet portfolios. These range from the office of prime minister and deputy prime minister to ministers of defense, foreign affairs, finance, and national security. The commander of the army and commander of the royal guard are also family. Members of the minority Sunni community, who make up an estimated 30 to 40 percent of the population, form the main pillar and primary constituency of the regime.

Although the uprising started out as nonsectarian in nature (as had Syria's), the Bahraini regime deliberately sectarianized it (as the Syrian regime did). The regime responded to a movement that demanded human rights and democracy as if it were one that wanted nothing more than Shi'i supremacy at the expense of Sunnis. As a result, members of the Sunni community circled their wagons in its defense.

Foreign intervention has played a critical role in determining the course of the uprisings in both Bahrain and Syria. The Saudi and Emirati soldiers and policemen who crossed the causeway linking Bahrain's main island with the mainland took up positions throughout the capital, Manama. This freed up the Bahraini military and security services (led by members of the ruling family and made up of Sunnis from Pakistan, Jordan, and elsewhere) to crush the opposition.

Having suppressed the uprising, the regime then embarked on a campaign of repression which was harsh by even Gulf standards. Regime opponents have faced mass arrests and torture in prison, demonstrations are banned, and insulting the king can result in a prison sentence of up to seven years. Security forces armed with riot gear have cordoned off rebellious Shi'i villages, terrorizing residents with nighttime raids. It is also illegal to possess a Guy Fawkes mask, the accessory of choice of anarchists and members of Occupy movements the world over. All the while, the regime has hidden behind the façade of a series of national dialogues whose outcomes it fixed.

While foreign intervention helped curtail the Bahraini uprising, it had the opposite effect in Syria. Iran, Russia, and Hizbullah have supported the regime. The West, Saudi Arabia, Qatar, Turkey, the opposition. Both sides have funneled arms and money to their proxies. Hizbullah fighters, Iranian soldiers, and Russian airmen and Special Forces have also joined the fray. This has not only served to escalate the violence, it created the environment in which ISIS could incubate before it set out to create its caliphate from portions of Iraq and Syria.

Why did the uprisings leave most Arab monarchies relatively unscathed?

There were no uprisings of significance in Qatar and the UAE. Those that broke out in the four of the seven remaining monarchies—Morocco, Saudi Arabia, Kuwait, and Oman— were never as regime threatening as those that broke out elsewhere. With the exception of the uprising in Bahrain (and, perhaps, Jordan), *protests* in the Arab monarchies share two important characteristics that set them apart from *uprisings* in the Arab republics: They have, for the most part, been more limited in scope, and they have demanded reform of the regime, not its overthrow.

It is not altogether clear why this discrepancy has been the case. Nor, for that matter, is it clear whether it will continue to be so. Some political scientists have argued that the reason the demand in monarchies has been for reform and not revolution is that monarchs have an ability that presidents—even presidents for life—do not have: They can retain executive power while ceding legislative power to an elected assembly and prime minister. As a result, the assembly and prime minister, not the monarch, become the focal point of popular anger when things go wrong. Unfortunately, this explanation rings hollow. While it might hold true for Kuwait, which has a parliament that can be, at times, quite raucous, Saudi Arabia does not even have a parliament and the king *is* the prime minister.

Others argue that oil wealth enables monarchs to buy off their opposition or prevent an opposition from arising in the first place. This might explain what happened in the Gulf monarchies, but Morocco (which had an uprising that the king enfeebled with a few cosmetic reforms) does not have oil. On the other hand, Bahrain—which has had a long history of rebellion and had a full-fledged uprising in 2011—is, when compared with Morocco, hydrocarbon rich.

It is entirely possible that in the future it will be necessary to reassess whether a monarchic category even exists. Bahrain was not the only monarchy in which opposition leaders called for the removal of the king. The same occurred in Jordan during demonstrations in November 2012. Although those demonstrations soon ran out of steam, there is no way to determine how deep the sentiment runs or whether it might re-emerge in the future. And while the world was focused on the anemic demonstrations of social-networking youths in Saudi Arabia's capital, violent protests, which met with violent repression, broke out in the predominantly Shiʻi Eastern Province of the country. Taking these latter protests into account challenges the notion that protests in the monarchies were limited in scope. Ultimately, the small number of monarchies included in this category (four out of eight in the region) makes any conclusions about a monarchic exception problematic.

What were protests in hybrid regimes like?

Iraq, Lebanon, and Palestine had a democratic façade when their protests broke out. The characteristics and objectives of the uprisings in all three reflected this. For example, populations had relative freedom to mass on the streets (often alongside disgruntled members of the ruling elite) and demand accountability from dysfunctional elected governments. Protests unfolded over time. And as governments proved unable or unwilling to break the political gridlock and answer even the most rudimentary needs of their populations, those populations expanded their demands to include an overhaul of the entire political system.

Demonstrations that began throughout Iraq on February 25, 2011 protested the lack of potable water, electrical shortages, and high unemployment. They then morphed into demonstrations that demanded the removal of oligarchs and an end to the sectarian system that guaranteed places in government based on sectarian identity. Weekly protests continued in Baghdad for years afterward. Demonstrations held in Beirut, Lebanon, four and a half years later protested the government's inability to remove garbage or provide other services (which secured for the campaign its evocative name, the "You Stink" movement). It followed a trajectory similar to the protest movement in Iraq. Neither movement has, to date, been able to remove or even move entrenched politicians.

A separate protest movement in Iraq began in winter 2014 in the Sunni areas of the country. Protesters demanded the end of discriminatory policies against their community perpetrated by the Shi'i government that the Americans had left behind after their withdrawal. The government met those protests with extreme violence (as it did the initial protests). This encouraged many Sunnis to sit on their hands or openly support ISIS when it began its conquests.

The Palestinian uprising took place in several stages. In January 2011, a group calling itself "Gaza Youth Breaks Out" issued its first manifesto, which stated, "There is a revolution growing inside of us, an immense dissatisfaction and frustration that will destroy us unless we find a way of canalizing this energy into something that can challenge the status quo and give us some kind of hope."[5]

That energy was "canalized" through the March 15 Youth Movement, a loose association of social-media-savvy young people similar to Egypt's April 6 Youth Movement. Like its predecessor, the March 15 Youth Movement began its protests with a "Day of Rage" in which tens of thousands of Palestinians took part. Rather than demand the ouster of the regime as their Egyptian counterparts had done, however, movement leaders demanded reconciliation between the two rival governments that ruled the West Bank and Gaza, respectively.

The final stage of the Palestinian uprising took place in the West Bank in September 2012 after the government raised prices on food and fuel. Spurred on by the same sort of labor activism that had proved decisive in the Egyptian uprising, protesters soon escalated their demands from the economic to the political: They called for the dismissal of the prime minister who led the West Bank government, the dismantling of that government, and the establishment of a Palestinian state with East Jerusalem as its capital, among other demands. The protest deeply shook the Palestinian leadership. It was then that it decided to seize the initiative and assuage public opinion by taking the case for Palestinian statehood to the General Assembly of the United Nations.

Were the Arab uprisings bound to fail?

For anyone watching the Egyptian uprising, it was difficult not to get caught up in the moment. Nevertheless, it is not unreasonable to ask how anyone could have thought that a regime as strong as the Egyptian—with its entrenched institutions and powerbrokers, its far-ranging patronage networks, its anti-democratic and oil-rich allies, its one-million-man army (including reserves) and two-million-man security apparatus—would throw in the towel after eighteen days without putting up more of a fight.

From the beginning, protesters and rebels throughout the Arab world faced overwhelming odds, foreign intervention, and extremist groups out for their own ends. Since participants in the uprisings were, more often than not, united by what they were against—the regime—rather than what they were for, they also disagreed among themselves about goals. In all cases but that of Libya (and, to a far lesser extent, Syria), they faced the indifference or hostility of the United States. Finally, the very spontaneity, leaderlessness, diversity, and loose organization on which the uprisings thrived proved to be their Achilles heel. True, these attributes kept regimes off balance and prevented them from reining in rebellious activity. But they also prevented protesters and rebels from agreeing on and implementing common tactics, strategy, and program.

There is one further factor that might have doomed the protests and uprisings to failure even had they been able to upturn or overthrow the old order: the wretched state of the economies of the non-oil-producing states and the absence of a blueprint other than the widely hated neo-liberalism to fix them. Throughout the region, economies went from bad to worse after uprisings broke out. This was the result of interrupted production, strikes, a lack of security that discouraged commerce and tourism, damage to infrastructure and sites of production, and displacement and migration.

In 2013, hundreds of thousands of Egyptians, angered by fuel shortages, electricity blackouts, and higher food prices, went out on the streets to demand that the incompetent but democratically elected president leave office. Most cheered on as the army first gave him an ultimatum, then arrested him and assumed power. It is entirely possible that the waning of public confidence in government that economic troubles bring might cause Tunisia's democratic experiment to come to grief as well.

What were the overall effects of the uprisings that began in 2010–2011?

To date, the scorecard for the uprisings that began in 2010 is disheartening. In Egypt and all the monarchies, the forces of reaction snuffed out the demands for change. Although the state system as a whole is not threatened—thanks in large measure to the support of both great and regional powers for the status quo—it is unlikely that the inhabitants of Libya, Yemen, and Syria will live under functioning governments that rule over the entirety of their territories anytime soon. Syria's bloodbath shows no sign of abating, Libya's and Yemen's might wind down only as a result of stalemate and exhaustion, and Iraqis now face more serious challenges, such as ISIS, than those that sparked the protests of 2011.

Across the region, there has been a rise in sectarianism, fueled by a combination of the Syrian civil war, the Iranian-Saudi rivalry over which regional power would determine the fate of embattled regimes and the regional order, and the Islamic State's war on everyone—including Shi'is—who does not follow the group's rigid interpretation of Islam or bow to its will. And however much protesters in Lebanon and Iraq might aspire to end sectarianism, once people have segregated themselves among "their own kind," or representation or employment opportunities have been allocated according to religious affiliation, sectarianism is unlikely to disappear.

In some states—Egypt, Bahrain, and much of the Arabian peninsula—populations face the heavier hand of regimes that, for a brief moment, had caught a glimpse of their own mortality. Elsewhere—Syria, Libya, Yemen, Iraq, even Tunisia and the Sinai—the weakening of regimes or the diversion of their attention elsewhere created an environment in which violent Islamist groups, from ISIS and al-Qaeda to Syria's Ahrar al-Sham and al-Qaeda affiliate Jabhat al-Nusra, might breed. Again, the Saudi-Iranian competition has made matters worse. In their efforts to combat the expansion of Iranian influence in the region and uphold Sunni dominance in the Arab world, Saudi Arabia and its Gulf allies have supported a number of violent Islamist groups on the battlefields of Syria and elsewhere. They have also financed mosques and schools that spread doctrines similar to those espoused by violent Islamists, thus normalizing those doctrines.

Since 2011, the region has experienced one humanitarian crisis after another. In the most brutal war zones—Syria, Libya, Yemen, Iraq—entire towns and cities have been laid waste, their populations scattered. War and civil disorder have not only taken their toll in terms of civilian casualties, but have also destroyed billions of dollars of infrastructure and created a public health nightmare. And particularly in Syria and Yemen, mass starvation—both a consequence and an intentional tool of war—is an ongoing threat, endangering millions.

Tunisia remains the one possible success story of the 2010–11 uprisings. Although the challenges it faces are daunting, it has thus far bucked the counterrevolution, repression, and violence experienced by many of its neighbors.

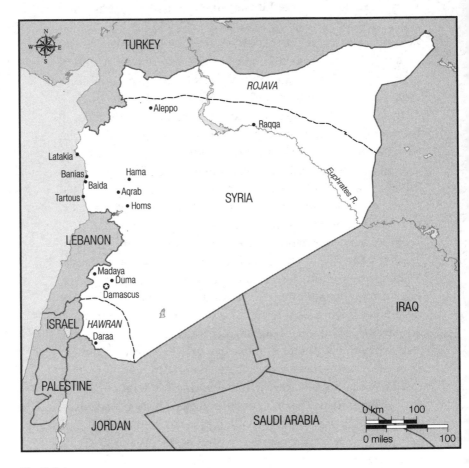

Map 2 Syria

3

THE SYRIA IMBROGLIO

How did the Syrian uprising begin?

The Syrian uprising has been going on for such a long time, and has engendered so much violence and destruction, that it is not easy to remember its beginnings. Those beginnings, as cliché would have it, were humble. In the first week of March 2011, Syrian security forces arrested ten schoolchildren aged fifteen or younger in the dusty provincial city of Daraa. The arrest came after the agents caught them writing "Down with the regime [*nizam*]"—a slogan borrowed from the Egyptian uprising—on a wall. The children were imprisoned and, while in prison, tortured. For about two weeks their families attempted to gain their release. Then they took to the streets. Security forces opened fire, killing several. The next day, their funeral procession brought out 20,000 demonstrators—in a city of 77,000—who chanted antigovernment slogans and attacked government buildings.

The government immediately understood the seriousness of the protests and sent out a delegation to meet with community members. The delegation heard their grievances, which by that time had expanded from the abducted children and the murder of their parents to economic and political demands. It promised to act on them. Soon after the meeting, however, security forces murdered fifteen worshippers at a local mosque, thus undercutting the delegation's attempt to defuse the crisis.

Coincidentally, protests erupted in the northern coastal city of Banias on the same day the anguished parents went out on the streets in Daraa. As in the case of the Daraa protests, the protests in Banias initially reflected local concerns (the secular regime had transferred female schoolteachers there who wore the *niqab*, the Syrian variant of the veil, to administrative jobs). Then, like their compatriots in Daraa, protesters expanded their focus to national issues, such as the brutality of the regime, the absence of democratic institutions, and corruption.

Protests soon spread to the coastal city of Latakia, then to Duma, north of the capital, where protesters aired similar grievances and met with the same violence. In village after village, town after town, protesters took to the streets as word spread of their neighbors' boldness and the regime's response. Eventually, protests reached the suburbs of Damascus and Syria's largest city, Aleppo. The Syrian uprising had begun.

How did the uprising in Syria differ from the uprisings in Tunisia and Egypt?

On March 15, every year since 2011, the Western media and members of the Syrian opposition commemorate the beginning of the Syrian uprising. The commemoration marks the date on which a group of protesters, calling themselves "Syrian Revolution 2011 against Bashar al-Assad," mounted a demonstration in Damascus, Syria's capital. The protesters were similar to those who occupied Tahrir Square in Cairo almost two months earlier. They were young, middle class, and social-media savvy. The protesters demanded, among other things, that the government rescind the emergency law and release political prisoners. The emergency law had been a thorn in the side of Syrian dissidents since it was enacted in 1963. It stripped Syrians of such fundamental rights as habeas corpus and the right to assemble. It also authorized extraordinary courts and granted even greater powers to the president.

The March 15 protest was not the first time opponents of the regime had organized that year. Sporadic protests had been going on since January. And like those other protests, attendance at the March 15 demonstration was anemic. It attracted only an estimated 200 to 350 protesters, and the security forces had no difficulty breaking it up. Then, four days later, all hell broke loose in Daraa and Banias.

Historians of the future will look to March 19—the date of the uprisings in Daraa and Banias—and not March 15 as the birth date of the Syrian uprising. This is important, because choosing one date over the other reframes subsequent developments. By choosing the earlier date, members of the Western media and the Syrian opposition have aligned the Syrian uprising with the Egyptian uprising (or, to be more precise, with the myth of the Egyptian uprising). In point of fact, however, the early days of the Syrian uprising more closely resemble those of the Libyan uprising than those of the uprisings in Egypt or Tunisia. This goes a long way toward explaining why the Syrian uprising turned out as it did.

The uprising in Syria differed from the Egyptian and Tunisian uprisings in four ways. First, there was no organization equivalent to the April 6 Movement to lead it. In fact, it wasn't led by any organization. Like the Libyan uprising, it was both spontaneous and leaderless. As a result, it suffered from all the problems that spontaneity and leaderlessness brings.

Second, the Syrian uprising had no epicenter like Egypt's Tahrir Square. As in the case of Libya, it broke out in the provinces. This explains why it was scattered and diffuse from its inception.

Furthermore, the Syrian uprising could not take advantage of associations autonomous from the government, such as the UGTT of Tunisia. The UGTT provided the Tunisian uprising with resources and a ready-made network of organizers who could mobilize crowds, give marching orders, and make plans on a national basis. In Syria, the General Federation of Trade Unions, the Syrian equivalent of the UGTT, operated as an arm of the ruling party. In addition, the government severely restricted other forms of association.

Finally, in Tunisia and Egypt the army stood down, then deposed dictators. It did so not because "The army and the people are one hand," as the Egyptian slogan went, but to save the regimes by decapitating them. In Syria, the army did not stand down. And although there were desertions, it did not fragment either, as had happened in Libya and Yemen. The army, led by Assad loyalists and relatives, remained fully committed to the survival of the regime and took the lead in the attempt to put down the uprising.

What was political and economic life like in Syria before the uprising?

Every year, Freedom House, an independent organization funded by the American government, publishes *Freedom in the World*, a country-by-country assessment of global political and civil rights. Freedom House's 2010 report on Syria begins a bit understated—"Syria is not an electoral democracy"[1]—but then turns scathing. Here are excerpts from the bill of indictment:

- The executive branch—the president and his inner circle—held all power.
- Members of the ruling Baath Party held most high government positions. They also dominated the rubber stamp parliament.
- Corruption was endemic. (Out of the 178 countries surveyed by Transparency International in 2010, Syria placed 127th.[2])
- The state owned all broadcast media and licensed all newspapers. This meant that the government could use the threat of license revocation to ensure that periodicals print the content it wanted.

- Syrians who possessed printed or recorded materials that had been banned were subject to arrest.
- Syrians could access the Internet only through state servers; the government blocked Facebook and YouTube, and reportedly monitored e-mail.
- Public demonstrations required official permission.
- A government ban prevented any group of five or more from discussing subjects that dealt with politics or the economy.
- Nongovernmental organizations had to register with the government.
- The Supreme State Security Court operated without regard to the constitution or the rights it guarantees. There was no appeal of its decisions.
- Police and security agencies regularly used torture to extract confessions and information from prisoners.
- The state held roughly 2,500 to 3,000 political prisoners, many of whom had never faced trial.
- Discrimination against the 10 percent of Syrians who were Kurds was officially sanctioned. The government banned the use of the Kurdish language.
- The government routinely denied those it deemed dangerous the right to foreign travel.
- The government monitored university classes, and professors faced firing for expressing opinions that were other than the Baath Party line.

When it came to economics, Syrians fared little better. In 2005, the Syrian government introduced what it called a "social market economy." The new policy was an acknowledgment on the part of the government that the stagnant Syrian economy needed shaking up. The government consulted with the IMF in drawing up the new economic blueprint, whose purpose was to shift Syria away from a command economy and closer to a free-market one. The result was an economy that combined the worst aspects of both systems. For example, privatization in Syria, as elsewhere, spawned a circle of crony capitalists who had privileged access to the government. The most notorious crony capitalist was Rami Makhlouf, the president's first cousin. He not only was the principal owner of the mobile communications giant, Syriatel, but also had holdings in real estate, transport, banking, insurance, construction, and tourism.

The social market economy yielded lackluster results. According to the IMF, in 2010 Syria's GDP (gross domestic product; that is, the total valuation of goods and services produced in Syria) grew by a mere 3 percent. Syria's own State Planning Commission estimated that the GDP would have to grow at an annual rate of 7 percent merely to absorb new job seekers. Thus it was that on the eve of the uprising, 67 percent of young males and 53 percent of young females in the labor pool were unemployed. On average, 81 percent of college graduates had to spend at least four years looking for work before landing their first job. Little wonder, then, that so many were disaffected.

Compounding Syrians' economic woes in the run-up to the uprising was global warming. From 2006 through 2010, Syria suffered from a drought of biblical proportions (scientists are divided as to whether it was the worst drought in 500 or 900 years). The drought devastated the Syrian countryside, where close to 60 percent of Syrians lived. Over its course, 75 percent of Syria's farms failed and 85 percent of Syria's livestock died. The drought sparked a rural-to-urban exodus of about 1.5 million Syrians. This helps explain why the birthplace and epicenters of the uprising were cities and towns surrounded by agricultural areas, such as Daraa and the towns in the Hawran region surrounding the capital.

Overall, according to numbers provided by the United Nations Development Programme,[3] when it came to measures of "human development"—life expectancy, educational attainment, political freedom, women's empowerment—Syria ranked among the bottom four states in the Arab world in 2010.

Who is Bashar al-Assad?

As hard as it is to believe now, before the uprising Bashar al-Assad enjoyed a reputation as a reformer. His father, Hafez al-Assad, who governed Syria from 1970 until his death in 2000, groomed Bashar's much despised elder brother to succeed him. When the brother died in an automobile accident, Hafez recalled Bashar from London, where he had been studying ophthalmology, and gave him a crash course in politics. After the elder Assad died, parliament amended the constitution, reducing the minimum age for president from forty to thirty-four—which was, not coincidentally, Bashar's exact age. Soon after acceding to power, Bashar oversaw the brief "Damascus Spring," a period of time when the government took a rather benign view of unsupervised political organizing and free expression. And when the Damascus Spring turned into the Damascus Winter, it was Hafez al-Assad's old cronies who took most of the blame.

How did the regime militarize the uprising?

The Syrian uprising differs from the others in three ways: the extent to which it became militarized, the extent to which it became sectarianized, and the extent to which it became a proxy war.

In the beginning, the regime depended most heavily on the security services to put down the uprising. The services broke up demonstrations and arrested protesters. While security personnel were effective where they were deployed, such tactics could not and did not prevent protests from leapfrogging from town to town, village to village.

In January 2012 the government shifted tactics. Realizing that its campaign to isolate and punish pockets of resistance using lightly armed security personnel had done little to stamp out the resistance, the regime brought in the heavy artillery—literally. The regime handed counterinsurgency over to the armed forces which, in the manner of militaries throughout the world, are more adept at wielding a meat cleaver than a scalpel.

Scorched-earth tactics were the order of the day. The test case proved to be the district of Baba Amr in the city of Homs, which called itself the capital of the revolution. Using all the firepower under its command—from tanks, helicopter gunships, and artillery, to snipers, mortars, and heavy machine guns—the army first cut off the city from the outside world, then softened up the rebel stronghold, reducing much of it to rubble. Finally, it stormed the district, killing about 250 rebels and driving the remainder out.

Its mission a success, the military began applying the same tactics elsewhere, escalating the level of violence with the occasional use of poison gas and barrel bombs (barrels filled with TNT that are dropped from the air indiscriminately). Partly as a result of these tactics, the government was able to regain the initiative. By 2014 it was in control of the line of cities that stretched from Damascus in the south to Aleppo in the north (although eastern Aleppo remained in rebel hands until December 2016). The government also dominated the coastal areas to the west, particularly those heavily populated by Alawites. Unable to seize control of much of the countryside and border areas, however, the government proved incapable of uprooting the resistance once and for all.

The military was not the only force that learned a lesson from the change in tactics. As it became increasingly clear that the brutality of the regime against its own citizens knew no bounds, the resistance also changed in form. At the outset, protests had been localized and, in large measure, peaceful affairs. Each rebel village or district had its own "local coordination committee." To protect demonstrations from informants and snipers, protesters staged rallies at night. Organized militias, made up of local fighters who had deserted from the Syrian army, provided further protection. This proved futile once the army replaced the security services as the regime's main tool to combat the uprising.

With their communities under siege or bombardment, local militias were often forced to retreat from their own neighborhoods, regroup, and fight wherever they sensed regime vulnerability. The close connection between local militias and their civilian counterparts thus ended, as did any restraint on the part of the military units that grew out of the militias. Civilians lost control of the uprising, and the balance of power within the opposition tipped in favor of the fighters.

A question that is frequently raised is why the opposition in Syria chose violent over nonviolent resistance. The answer is simple: They didn't—violence was chosen for them.

How did the regime sectarianize the uprising?

The ruling elites of Syria were bound together through ties of family and sect. This effectively coup-proofed the regime. To paraphrase Benjamin Franklin, if they did not hang together, they would all hang separately. Rule by members of a minority sect also affected the way the ruling elite approached members of the broader Alawite community and members of other minority groups (Christians make up about 10 percent of the Syrian population, and there are other minority groups in Syria as well). Because the regime was identified with a minority sect, it could count on the support of members of that and other minority groups who feared massacre at the hands of the majority Sunni population should the government fall. The United Nations' Regional Bureau for Arab States calls this dynamic "legitimacy of blackmail"[4] (more properly rendered "legitimacy by blackmail"): Stick by us or they'll kill you.

The uprising had begun without reference to sectarian identity. Protesters focused on the removal of a repressive and corrupt regime. In fact, before the uprising Syrian society as a whole was not polarized around sectarian identities; rather, it was united through the bonds of what one social scientist has called a "public civility." Members of various religious groups of course recognized their religious differences and, in the privacy of their homes, might have made derogatory comments about one another. But they mingled with members of other religious groups in markets, public schools, coffee shops, and on public transportation. The regime therefore deliberately set out to polarize Syrian society—and the uprising—into opposing sectarian camps.

The regime adopted a number of tactics to accomplish this. As soon as the uprising broke out, the regime labeled its opponents salafis, Islamists, terrorists, jihadis, and agents of Saudi Arabia, among other things. (The term "jihadi," in its current usage, refers to a Sunni Muslim committed to waging violent *jihad*, or struggle, against non-Muslims or those they consider non-Muslim. Jihadis are a variety of Islamist.) To ensure this would be a self-fulfilling prophecy, as early as spring 2011 the regime released salafis, Islamists, and jihadis, including those associated with al-Qaeda, from prison. Many ended up in the al-Qaeda affiliate in Syria, Jabhat al-Nusra (the Support Front), or in ISIS. (In July 2016, Jabhat al-Nusra changed its name to Jabhat Fateh al-Sham—the Front for Victory in [Greater] Syria—and ended its formal affiliation with al-Qaeda.)

The regime also polarized society through violence. It organized armed "popular committees" to protect Alawite villages, and it equipped pro-regime vigilantes with knives and clubs for use in street battles with mostly unarmed protesters. And it used the dreaded *shabiha* (a word related to the Arabic word for "ghosts")—ninja-clad Alawite thugs who hailed from Assad's home town and its immediate vicinity—to provoke tit-for-tat violence against Sunnis. In July 2011, nine died in Homs after an Alawite mob surrounded a Sunni mosque in one of the first recorded instances of sectarian conflict during the uprising. That was just a harbinger of worse to come: In Baida and Banias, for example, shabiha massacred 248 Sunnis, and in the village of Aqrab opposition fighters slaughtered at least 125 Alawites.

What foreign assistance has the Syrian government received?

Outside powers have intervened in the Syrian civil war both on the side of the government and on the side of the opposition. This has not only made the war bloodier, it has prolonged it.

Iran, Hizbullah, and Russia are the main allies of the Syrian government. Although rulers of Syria and Iran are both Shi'is (Alawites were acknowledged as part of the broader Shi'i community in 1974), the Iranian-Syrian alliance has nothing to do with shared religious affiliation or ideology. The Iranian-Syrian alliance began in 1981 during the Iran-Iraq war, when, in a brilliant strategic move, Hafez al-Assad became the only Arab leader to side with Iran. All of a sudden a medium-sized state with a weak economy became an important regional player as both Iraq's allies and Iran courted its favor, offering Syria political and financial inducements either to switch sides or stay where it was. The Iranians, recognizing a propaganda coup when they saw one, were particularly generous, providing Syria with discounted oil and debt relief.

The alliance with Iran bolstered Syria's anti-imperialist reputation. It also increased the price it could exact from the United States (which secretly backed Iraq in the war) for making peace with Israel. In return, the Syria connection enabled Iran to earn the cachet of a regional power whose field of operations stretched from the Mediterranean to the Gulf.

Since the outbreak of the uprising, Iran has provided the Syrian regime with intelligence and has sent advisers who have instructed the Syrian military on tactics and on controlling cyberspace (techniques that the Iranians perfected putting down their own antigovernment protests—the "Green Revolution" of 2009). It has assisted and supplied weapons to paramilitary units such as the shabiha and the popular committees, and has even deployed irregular forces made up of its own citizens, Afghans, and Iraqis. It has established an air bridge which resupplied the Syrian army with ammunition, weapons, and even refurbished attack helicopters. And Iran has sent combat troops to assist the Syrian regime. At one point, there were more than 3,000 Iranian soldiers from the Islamic Revolutionary Guard Corps and its elite Quds Force fighting in Syria.

Hizbullah has a huge stake in ensuring the survival of the Syrian regime. Syria provides a vital supply route that stretches from Iran to Lebanon, assuring a steady resupply of arms and equipment to a group that has repeatedly come into conflict with Israel. Because it comprises a popular militia, Hizbullah possesses a level of expertise vital to the training of the pro-regime popular committees that protect Alawite and Shi'i villages in Syria. And unlike Iranians, members of Hizbullah have the added advantage of being native speakers of Arabic.

The final element that makes up the pro-regime camp is Russia. The Russian-Syrian alliance is long-standing, stretching back to the 1950s—the Soviet era. Because of the alliance, Russia has been able to project its power into the region, and its naval base in the Syrian port city of Tartous enables it to do likewise in the eastern Mediterranean. There is also an intangible component to Russia's embrace of the Syrian regime after the outbreak of the uprising: It allows Russia to poke a thumb in the American eye. At a time when President Obama's detractors accused the president (wrongly) of throwing Hosni Mubarak under a bus, Russian president Vladimir Putin bragged that Russia stands by its friends. And at a time when the only options for the United States in Syria seemed to be bad ones, causing it to dither, the Russians could apply a legally sanctioned muscular policy in defense of a sovereign government.

Like Iran, Russia provides Syria with weapons. As of 2014, Russia had contracted for close to 5 billion dollars' worth of arms to sell to the Syrian government. (After Russia displayed how those weapons could turn the tide on the Syrian battlefield a year later, economists predicted global orders for Russian weapons would increase by $6 to 7 billion). Like Iran and Hizbullah, Russia has sent advisers who work closely with the Syrian military. And like its allies, Russia has participated directly in combat. Not only have Russian warplanes flown missions in support of the Syrian army, Russia has deployed Special Forces and artillery and tank units to back it up as well. Russian intervention saved the regime in autumn 2015 when it appeared that the opposition had the Syrian army on the ropes.

Most important, Russia has provided the Syrian regime with diplomatic cover. Russia has blocked numerous UN Security Council resolutions that condemned actions taken by the Syrian regime. Russia also came up with the plan to remove chemical weapons from Syria (thereby rendering moot the debate in the United States about possible military action to punish Syria for their use) and supported the Syrian position during the various rounds of negotiations between the Syrian government and the opposition.

Who supports the opposition?

The West, including the United States, along with Saudi Arabia, Qatar, and Turkey, acting alone, in ad hoc groupings, or in concert, have been the principal supporters of the opposition (in 2016, Turkey, having decided that resolving its Kurdish predicament was more important than further alienating its neighbor, shifted toward a more conciliatory stance toward the Syrian regime). When they act in concert they act through the Friends of Syria group. The group, founded in 2012 to do an end run around Russian (and Chinese) veto power in the United Nations Security Council, comprised, at its inception, 114 states (over the years it has grown considerably smaller). In addition to enabling its members to speak with a single voice and coordinate their military and humanitarian assistance, its major accomplishment was to midwife the creation of the National Coalition for Syrian Revolutionary and Opposition Forces (called the Syrian National Coalition, or SNC, for short).

The SNC is, at least on paper, the supreme coordinating body recognized by most of the international community as

the sole legitimate political representative of a unified opposition. Its purpose is to enable foreign powers to channel assistance to "moderate" opposition forces efficiently, coordinate
the efforts of politicians who mainly reside outside Syria with
military commanders on the ground, and enable the opposition to speak with a single voice in international councils. It
has also participated in international negotiations aimed at
ending the Syrian civil war. Consisting mainly of exiles, the
SNC has little influence in Syria, where the various armed
groups hold sway.

Since the uprising is in the hands of those armed groups, the
main focus of states that back the opposition has been military.
Like the states supporting the Assad government, those that
support the opposition have armed, trained, and provided
logistical support to their clients. They have also financed
them. But states that back the opposition have not been nearly
as effective as those that back the Syrian government.

There are two reasons for this. First, some, mostly Western,
states are reluctant to supply the opposition with some of the
most effective matériel, such as MANPADS (man-portable
air-defense systems, or shoulder-launched surface-to-air missiles). They fear that advanced weaponry might fall into the
wrong hands, such as jihadis fighting the government (Saudi
Arabia and Qatar are not so squeamish). Opposition militias
are constantly splintering and reforming. They are intermixed
on the battlefield, so by providing weaponry to a "moderate"
group a jihadi group might be advantaged as well.

There is another reason why states are reluctant to supply
the opposition with certain weapons systems: "Moderate"
groups have proved not only to be feckless on the battlefield,
but untrustworthy off it. In 2015, for example, a US-aligned
group, the Southern Front, sold the weapons it bought with
American money to the Yarmouk Martyrs Brigade, a group
with suspected ISIS ties. About a year later, the United States
blocked Turkey from arming and providing logistical support
to one of the few opposition groups with a Syria-wide reach

because of the group's salafi agenda. The United States, by the way, supplied MANPADS to the Afghan rebels fighting Soviet invaders in the 1980s. The result was the Taliban, al-Qaeda, and 9/11.

The second reason pro-regime states have been more effective than pro-opposition ones is that the former are united by a single goal—maintain the Assad regime—while the goals of the latter are all over the place. Sure, they all want to get rid of Assad and his cohort. But what then? Saudi Arabia supports some pretty unsavory groups, including Jaysh al-Islam (the Army of Islam) and Ahrar al-Sham (the Free Men of Syria), whose ideology is not all that different from the former al-Qaeda affiliate, Jabhat Fateh al-Sham. Both want Syria to be guided by a strict interpretation of Islamic Law. Turkey's overriding goal is to prevent the emergence of an independent or even autonomous Kurdish state in northern Syria that might inspire Turkey's own Kurds to follow the same path. Turkey thus blackballed the participation of any Syrian Kurdish group in the international conference held in 2016 to discuss Syria's future, and sent its military into northern Syria to divide Kurdish controlled areas from one another.

Like Saudi Arabia and Turkey, the United States wants to see Assad gone. But the United States learned lessons from Iraq 2003 and Libya 2011. In both places, the United States had promoted regime change and a thorough housecleaning. In both places, the results were disastrous. Both states descended into chaos. Unlike Saudi Arabia, therefore, the United States has been more interested in brokering a negotiated settlement that would leave parts of the regime—particularly those that might ensure internal stability—largely intact. It certainly does not want to replace it with some ISIS knockoff. And since the American priority in Syria is the destruction of ISIS there, and since Syrian Kurds have been playing a vital role in achieving that end, the United States has not wished to see its Kurdish partners sidelined. Because the main Syrian Kurdish group is closely aligned with the Turkey-based Kurdistan Workers'

Party (PKK)—an insurgent group which is on the US State Department's list of terrorist organizations—Turkey does.

How has foreign intervention prolonged Syria's agony?

At the beginning of 2015, the Syrian civil war was, in the words of the *New York Times*, a "chaotic stalemate."[5] Neither the government nor the opposition forces arrayed against it were able to gain the upper hand. Battlefield gains were reversed, regained, then reversed again. Battles fought between the two sides more closely resembled a war of attrition than a war of movement.

By summer 2015, the situation on the battlefield had completely shifted in the rebels' favor. In 2014, the United States, Jordan, and Saudi Arabia had set up a joint Military Operations Command (MOC) in Amman, Jordan. Commonly known as the "operations room," MOC collected intelligence, financial and logistical assistance, and military know-how from the United States and Saudi Arabia. It then coordinated the flow of information and assistance to opposition groups fighting on the southern front in Syria. MOC, in effect, unified the operations of those groups not only on a tactical level, but on a strategic one as well. The coordinated effort MOC directed assured their victory in the "Southern Storm" campaign, which led to the rebel seizure of a vital Jordanian-Syrian border crossing.

Opposition groups throughout Syria began copying MOC by setting up their own operations rooms. This enabled them to wage major campaigns that spun out over time. By autumn 2015 the Syrian army was reeling. The opposition had pushed it back to a defensive line that was steadily shrinking. Then the reversal was itself reversed.

In July 2015, Bashar al-Assad made a formal request to Vladimir Putin, asking for direct Russian intervention to fight "jihadi terror" in Syria. The Russians responded by sending in warplanes, tanks, and artillery a month later. Russian operations continued for months thereafter, in spite of the fact that Putin announced that he had achieved his goals. Russian jets, artillery, and even cruise missiles pounded opposition positions—jihadi, Islamist, and non-Islamist alike (however much the Russians tried to deny it, initially 85 percent of Russian targets were non-ISIS related). As a result, the Syrian army regained both the initiative and territory, particularly in the north and along the vital Damascus-Aleppo highway. Massive, indiscriminant Russian bombing enabled the Syrian government to retake eastern Aleppo, the opposition's most important redoubt. Once again, foreign intervention had changed the course of the Syrian civil war.

Political scientists argue that negotiations among parties involved in a civil war—the most common sort of war since the end of the Period of Decolonization—can succeed in ending hostilities only when each side views a battlefield victory as impossible and continued warfare as injurious to itself as to its opponents. They call this a "mutually hurting stalemate." If one side or the other thinks its goals can be achieved on the battlefield, however, there is little possibility of reaching a settlement. After all, why compromise if there is still the possibility of taking it all? Only after both sides in a civil war realize there is no possibility of achieving their goals through violence is the time ripe for negotiations (political scientists call this, cleverly, "ripeness theory"). They point to a number of examples of civil strife—in Northern Ireland, Bosnia, and elsewhere—that, they claim, proves this.

Foreign intervention in a civil war makes it difficult to achieve a mutually hurting stalemate and thus makes it difficult to achieve ripeness. Losing belligerents will naturally look to their foreign patrons to help them turn the tide. And those patrons are usually only too willing to help. Foreign backers of each side view the stakes not only in terms of a winning or losing proxy, but also in the wider, more critical context that made them get involved in someone else's war in the first place. Both Saudi Arabia and Iran view the Syrian civil war as one front in their battle for regional dominance. They are unlikely, therefore, simply to throw up their hands at the first signs of setback. Rather, under such circumstances they are more likely to ramp up their level of assistance to their proxies. When they do, their opponent is likely to do the same, thus increasing the level of violence and further delaying the ripe time.

Who is the Syrian opposition?

The Syrian opposition is united in its goal of removing Bashar al-Assad. And although its various elements have cooperated on the battlefield, they see eye to eye on little more. For example, the opposition in Syria is ideologically diverse (when it is ideological at all). This only stands to reason, since Syrians themselves are ideologically diverse and there has been an influx of ideologically committed foreign fighters (particularly jihadis) into Syria. In addition, groups often adopt the ideology of their paymaster, be it Turkey, Qatar, or Saudi Arabia, to maintain their funding or lifeline to weapons. Most observers consider neither ISIS nor the Kurdish People's Protection Units (YPG) that is fighting ISIS part of the opposition. Neither is focused on overthrowing the regime.

By summer 2016 there were more than 100,000 opposition fighters divided among a significant number of groups. It is not easy keeping track of them: They have been highly fractious. Some have dissolved under internal or external pressure. Others joined in various coalitions that all too often are ephemeral. Thus, the Syrian Islamic Liberation Front (founded September 2012)—a coalition of Islamist militias—morphed into the Syrian Islamic Front (December 2012), which, in turn, morphed into the Islamic Front (September 2013) as conditions changed, groups left or joined or were blackballed, and rival outside powers such as Saudi Arabia and Qatar played their hands. Some groups consist of no more than a few dozen men; others number in the tens of thousands. Most of them operate locally: Of the close to 150 groups listed in an Institute for the Study of War report published in October 2015,[6] fewer than a third had a presence in more than one governorate (province), and about half of those were located in only two.

The first armed group out of the box was the Free Syrian Army (FSA). The FSA originally consisted of deserters from the regular Syrian army who, in the early days of the uprising, banded together on a local level to protect demonstrators from snipers deployed by the regime. When the regime changed tactics and militarized the uprisings, it forced FSA fighters into the countryside, where they regrouped. Over time, moderate Islamist fighters joined the non-Islamist deserters in the FSA as well.

From the get-go the FSA suffered from an ineffective command structure, corrupt leadership, shifting ideological winds, and the superior capabilities and experience of hardcore Islamist fighters (as Obama put it, militias like the FSA consisted of "former farmers or teachers or pharmacists"[7]). Most important, the FSA suffered from spotty American support and commitment. Strangely, there is little agreement on its fate. Some observers deny it still exists as a cohesive force or claim that Russian airstrikes devastated its ranks. Others put its numbers at 20,000 to 30,000. Still others say its various brigades have been integrated into the Southern Front, which carved out the liberated zone on the Jordanian border in 2015.

Without doubt the most effective opposition groups currently fighting in Syria are on the jihadi end of the Islamist spectrum. The largest is Harakat Ahrar al-Sham al-Islamiyya (the Islamic Movement of the Free Men of Syria, commonly called, simply, Ahrar al-Sham), which fields an estimated 20,000 fighters. Because it wants to establish an Islamic state in Syria, it has received support from Qatar and Saudi Arabia, with which it is ideologically attuned. Turkey has also supported it, mainly to buy influence. Although it has links to al-Qaeda and has committed atrocities, it has been effective in the fight against Bashar al-Assad. This is the reason the United States has balked at putting it on the State Department list of terrorist organizations.

The State Department had no such compunctions about Jabhat al-Nusra/Jabhat Fateh al-Sham, a group that worked in concert with Ahrar al-Sham in northwest Syria. They founded, along with five other groups, the operations-room-based Army of Conquest (Jaysh al-Fatah). The army was so successful in 2015 that it goaded Bashar al-Assad to solicit direct Russian intervention in the Syrian civil war.

Jabhat al-Nusra was founded in 2012 by Syrian members of the Islamic State in Iraq (ISI), the precursor to ISIS. While the leadership of ISI viewed the Syrian civil war as a sideshow, it did allow a number of its fighters to return home to fight to depose Bashar al-Assad. They soon asserted their autonomy from ISI and affiliated with al-Qaeda, although their ideology represents the antithesis of al-Qaeda's. That which makes al-Qaeda unique among jihadi groups is that it ignores local despots. Instead, it focuses its attention on the "far enemy"—the Soviet Union or the United States, for example. According to al-Qaeda, there is no point in bothering with the puppet when it is the puppetmaster who counts. Jabhat al-Nusra, on the other hand, fought (and continues to fight, under its new name) to overthrow Bashar al-Assad. The rebranding of Jabhat al-Nusra therefore had nothing to do with ideology. Its purpose was to make the group more palatable to other groups and foreign governments. It didn't.

According to the Syrian Network for Human Rights, the regime was responsible for 75 percent of the casualties Syrians suffered in 2015. Of these, 76 percent were civilians, and 38 percent of those casualties were women and children. That's what barrel bombs and artillery barrages in civilian areas will do (ISIS was responsible for about 13 percent of casualties). Nevertheless, the picture of the Syrian civil war cannot be painted in black and white. Rebel groups have also been responsible for the suffering of the Syrian population.

In a 2015 report,[8] Amnesty International documented twenty-four cases of abduction by armed opposition groups, the use of torture, the imposition of harsh penalties purportedly sanctioned by Islamic law, summary executions, and the killing of civilians in two "liberated" governorates alone over a three-year period. In March 2016, fighters from Ahrar al-Sham and Jabhat al-Nusra raided the Alawite village of al-Zahraa, killing nineteen and abducting 120. Elsewhere, opposition groups have imposed harsh exactions on the civilian population. In the words of one observer commenting on the competition among various groups for control over the oil, wheat, and border crossings that come with the territory they fight over, "opposition-held Syria is Mad Max meets The Sopranos."[9] The violence and racketeering is not limited to jihadis or even to Islamist members of the opposition; non-Islamists participate as well.

How bad is the damage to Syria?

In February 2016—one month before the fifth anniversary of the Syrian uprising—the Syrian Centre for Policy Research (SCPR) released the latest in a series of reports about the impact of the Syrian civil war on the lives of Syrians and on the Syrian social fabric. The document was titled, "Syria Confronting Fragmentation! Impact of Syrian Crisis Report."[10] The exclamation point in the title clearly reflects both the alarm felt by the authors and the urgency they wished to convey. So do the statistics they provide. Here are some of them:

- By the end of 2015, there were 470,000 war-related deaths. Syrians with war-related injuries numbered 1.9 million. This means that 11.5 percent of the prewar population ended up as casualties.
- The war had uprooted about 45 percent of the population. Among them were 6.36 million who were internally displaced, 3.11 million refugees, and 1.17 migrants (economic refugees).
- The overall poverty rate was 85.2 percent. About 69.3 percent of the poor lived in "absolute poverty" (a condition of severe deprivation). About 35 percent were in danger

of slipping into "abject poverty" (in which they would be unable to meet their basic food needs).
- Life expectancy at birth dropped about fifteen years.
- In 2011 unemployment had been 14.9 percent; by the end of 2015 it was 52.9 percent.
- Of those working, more than one third participated in the "conflict economy" as fighters, suppliers, smugglers, and the like.
- Around 45.2 percent of children no longer attended school.
- The total economic loss as a result of the conflict, through the end of 2015, was estimated to be $254.7 billion, mainly because of drops in production and the destruction of plants and equipment. (Other reports put the damage to infrastructure—highways, bridges, airfields, high voltage power lines—at $180 to 200 billion.)

Since the release of the report, the situation in Syria has only become worse. By the beginning of 2017, it was estimated that unemployment had hit 58 percent, that half of all Syrian children did not attend school, and that life expectancy had dropped twenty years. In other words, the statistics are trending in an alarming direction, and in some cases, that trending is rapid.

Statistics can, of course, convey only so much. They fail to express fully what Syrians have experienced on a daily basis. For example, forced displacement, along with malnutrition resulting from the Syrian government's use of starvation as a weapon of war, has created a public health disaster. Diseases that had been under control—including typhoid, tuberculosis, rabies, Hepatitis A, and cholera—are under control no longer. Diseases that had been eradicated, such as polio, have returned. According to the World Health Organization, in 2010 polio had existed in only three countries in the world: Nigeria, Afghanistan, and Pakistan. In all likelihood, jihadis traveling to Syria from Afghanistan and Pakistan to fight were responsible for reintroducing the disease.

Polio is a disease commonly associated with children, and by March 2014 that segment of the population had been particularly hard hit. About half of all refugees were children who, like the children trapped in the war zones, not only went without schooling, but had little access to regular medical care and immunizations. According to one poll conducted in a refugee camp, three out of four children there had lost a loved one. About half of them suffered from post-traumatic stress disorder or depression.

Then there is the fraying of the social fabric. As might be inferred from the statistics, the uprising transformed the physical face of Syria and with it the ties that had bound communities together. According to the SCPR report, the physical destruction of communities created a "state of alienation and fragmentation . . . pushing the majority of people to act against their own benefit and contrary to the aspirations of their community."[11]

During the first five years of the uprising, fighting destroyed about two million of 4.7 million homes. Barrel bombs and artillery bombardment reduced entire neighborhoods to rubble. And both sides, particularly the government, engaged in what can only be described as sectarian cleansing. Here is how one activist described Homs three years into the uprising:

Once a thriving city of approximately 700,000, [Homs] is today a broken ruin. The regime loyalist Alawi-majority districts are today the only areas of the city where normal life continues. Regime bombs have fallen relentlessly every day on the rest of the city, destroying apartment buildings, shops, and historic mosques. Entire districts, such as Khalidiya, Baba Amr, Jourat al Shiah, Bayada and Warsha have been emptied of their inhabitants and completely destroyed. Many of Homs's residents have fled from the centre of the city to the outer suburbs, such as Wa'r, which has taken in at least 200,000 refugees and is completely surrounded by the regime. Others are now outside the city or outside the country. In the Old City, not a single building remains intact and the siege on the inhabitants was complete and total. ... No food was allowed to enter—starvation and deaths from treatable injuries were the norm. Residents had to bring in their food from under the sewers to avoid starvation.

"The Syrian revolution began with protests calling for freedom, democracy, and dignity," he concludes, "but it could end with a nightmare of sectarian cleansing and genocide."[12]

How has the Syrian uprising affected Syria's neighbors?

Syria abuts Turkey, Iraq, Jordan, Israel, and Lebanon and its uprising has affected its neighbors in a number of ways. There is, for example, the threat that one or more might be pulled directly into the fighting. Turkey has already been: Turkish troops crossed into Syria in August 2016, ostensibly to root out ISIS, and did so again that November to "remove Assad" (whatever the official explanation, it was Turkey's alarm at Kurdish gains that, in fact, triggered both incursions). And Israel has launched attacks on convoys and installations that appeared to threaten it directly or, through the transfer of weapons and materiel to Hizbullah, indirectly. In addition, both Jordan and Iraq were forced to take defensive action after deliberate or accidental Syrian army provocations and after armed gangs attempted to infiltrate their territory from Syria.

The Syrian civil war also created the toxic environment in which ISIS thrived. ISIS has made much of Iraq into a war zone, reignited Iraq's own Kurdish question, and sparked the mass exodus of minorities to safer havens both inside the country and abroad.

Refugees from Syria have placed an enormous strain on the resources of neighboring states and exported Syria's sectarian troubles to those states. By summer 2016 there were

4.8 million refugees registered with the United Nations High Commissioner for Refugees in the region. The largest number were in Turkey (about 2.7 million), followed by Lebanon (more than one million), and Jordan (close to 660,000)—and those were just the ones registered.

To get a sense of what the influx of refugees means, take the (admittedly extreme) case of Lebanon, a country which, in normal times, had a population of 4.4 million. Syrian refugees thus make up approximately a quarter of Lebanon's inhabitants. The equivalent number of refugees in the case of the United States would be more than 73 million. In 2015 the United States admitted one of the largest cohorts of refugees it had ever admitted: 70,000. At the time, the American economy was more than 400 times larger than Lebanon's. (In early 2017, the Trump administration sought to place an indefinite ban on all Syrian refugees seeking asylum in the US.)

By summer 2016, the Turkish government claimed to have spent $7.5 billion for refugee assistance. The Lebanese and Jordanian governments spend $4.5 billion and $2.5 billion annually. The international community does pick up some of the tab. Nevertheless, the burden for providing municipal services (such as lighting, road building, and the delivery of clean water), along with healthcare and educational services, falls heavily on host countries.

There are other burdens as well. In Jordan, for example, many of the refugees who crossed the border early on did not end up in camps. Instead, they ended up living with relatives in cities and towns in the north of the country. Refugees in other states acted similarly, although their numbers were not as great. The influx of refugees not living in camps drives up real estate prices, contributes to inflation, and creates tensions with local populations who fear that refugees entering the job market threaten their livelihoods (in reality, most refugees who find jobs work as unskilled laborers, performing tasks citizens of their host countries consider menial). According to the International Labor Organization, the influx of refugees sparked a doubling of Lebanon's unemployment rate (to 20 percent), increased the number of Lebanese living below the poverty line by 170,000, and caused an additional $7.5 billion in economic losses—and that was in 2013, toward the beginning of the Syrian civil war.

The uprising in Syria created a unique refugee problem for Iraq. In addition to hosting Syrians, Iraq also found itself hosting Iraqi refugees who had fled to Syria with the onset of sectarian conflict in Iraq after the 2003 American invasion and occupation. They then returned to avoid the same dangers in their place of refuge. They are called Iraq's "doubly displaced." With Iraq once again a war zone, it is apparent their travails have not ended.

The spillover effect of Syria's sectarian conflict has not only affected states with significant histories of sectarian strife— Lebanon and Iraq—it has affected Turkey as well. In Lebanon, 2013 was payback time for Hizbullah's decision to stand with and fight for the Assad regime. Militant (Sunni) Islamists from Syria followed Hizbullah fighters back to Lebanon, attacking them and their offices so often that the fighters had to set up their own "popular committees" to protect their home towns and neighborhoods. In the coastal city of Tripoli, Sunni and Shi'i gangs—the former supporting the Syrian opposition, the latter the Syrian government—clashed on an almost weekly basis. Syrian army deserters found sanctuary in the predominantly Sunni northern border area of Lebanon, where they threatened Hizbullah's forces in Syria from the rear and where they, too, have clashed with local Shi'is and Hizbullah supporters. Tensions in Lebanon rose so high that the government postponed the 2013 parliamentary elections, fearing an escalation in violence that would accompany electioneering and either losses or gains by Hizbullah's electoral wing.

Iraq faces its worst sectarian crisis since 2008 for two reasons. First, the Syrian-Iraqi border is porous, allowing militant (Sunni) Islamists freedom of movement across wide, unpoliced terrain, sometimes fighting against regime forces on the Syrian side of the border, sometimes fighting against the Shi'i-dominated Iraqi government on the other side.

In addition, the Sunni population of Iraq, concentrated in the area to the northwest of Baghdad, is a minority (Shi'is make up 60 to 65 percent of the population of Iraq), subject to discrimination and abuse by the government. Sunnis found inspiration in the actions of their coreligionists in Syria. In winter 2013, they began mounting a series of antigovernment demonstrations, which led Iraqis down the same path previously trod by Syrians: The government, linking the protest organizers to former president Saddam Hussein, met them with repression. This, in turn, moved Sunni tribal leaders to form a tribal army, which militarized the protest movement. What had begun as peaceful protests ended up as an insurgency, replete with car bombings and assassinations. Repression by the Iraqi government was one of the reasons a number of Sunnis chose to support ISIS in the immediate aftermath of its military foray into Iraq in 2014.

One does not usually associate Turkey with sectarian problems (it is most noted for its Kurdish question). But it, too, has experienced a rise in sectarian tensions as a result of the Syrian uprising. Two minority groups in particular came to resent the Turkish government's early anti-Assad stance, its willingness to support Sunni extremists in Syria, and the influx of mostly Sunni refugees from Syria into the areas they inhabit. They are Turkish Alevis, who comprise 10 to 20 percent of the population, and Alawites, who are mainly of Arab descent with strong ties to their Syrian coreligionists (and yes, their names are not the only difference between the two groups). Beginning in 2013, protests and clashes between members of both communities and police, as well as bombings, heightened tensions in southern Turkey. And to top matters off, Syrian Kurds fleeing ISIS began arriving in Turkey in droves in late September 2014.

How will the Syrian civil war end?

There are four possible outcomes to the Syrian civil war: The Syrian regime or the opposition wins an out-and-out victory on the battlefield; Syria is divided; there is a negotiated settlement; or the conflict continues, with periods of greater or lesser violence among the various parties.

Of the four scenarios, the first and second are least likely. The first is unlikely because the Syrian conflict is a proxy war. In terms of the second, there are two possible ways to envision the division of Syria. The first is that Syria fragments as a result of violence and battlefield stalemate. This would leave the Syrian government in charge of the territory stretching from the Damascus-Aleppo line west, a Kurdish government ruling over a territory running west to east on the Turkish border, and various opposition groups controlling territory elsewhere (assuming, as is probable, that ISIS will be destroyed in Syria).

Such a forced division is improbable, mainly because the international community is unlikely to countenance it. Since Syria is in such a dangerous neighborhood, its breakup would create problems for its neighbors, not to mention the fact that jihadi groups would likely use one or more "liberated" zones as a safe haven. The United States certainly would not support it, nor would Russia (unless it were the only way to maintain a friendly government in the area). And Turkey would not stomach an independent Rojava (Kurdish for Western Kurdistan) on its southern border.

But what if Syria is partitioned in a negotiated settlement? This would enable the Alawites in the west to organize their own affairs, the Kurds theirs, and the Sunnis theirs. And, to get around Turkish objections to an independent Kurdistan, there is always the possibility of linking Syrian territories in some form of federation, like what the Iraqi constitution guarantees for its sub-national units.

Setting aside, for the moment, the fact that Iraq hardly provides a model for any state to emulate, a negotiated division of Syria is also improbable for a number of reasons. First, with the single exception of the Druze—a small ethnoreligious group which, for the most part, lives in the country's southwest—there are no compact minorities in Syria (compact minorities are minorities that live together in a well-defined territory and form a vast majority of its population). Instead, minority populations are scattered or live in regions that are ethnically and religiously mixed.

For example, while Alawites easily form a majority of the inhabitants of the Latakia governorate in the west, they make up only about 50 percent of the inhabitants of the governorate's capital, also called Latakia. Likewise, the so-called Kurdish region in the northeast. Beginning in 1965, Syrian governments began moving Arabs into the area and deporting Kurds out for security reasons. As a result, establishing separate states or a federation of autonomous statelets would set off a spate of ethnic cleansing the likes of which Syrians have yet to experience.

There are other roadblocks to negotiating a division of Syria as well. Not only do foreign powers not want the division to occur, a vast majority of Syrians don't either. They don't even want the more modest federal scheme, because most view federalization as a precursor to division. And then there is the problem of drawing the borders of the new statelets. Each would want to maximize the territory under its control, particularly if it meant gaining access to resources like oil. This is the reason that the Iraqi state and the Kurdistan regional government were never able to decide in whose territory the city of Kirkuk lay. After years of haggling, the Kurds just took it when the Iraqi central government was preoccupied with fighting ISIS.

This leaves two possible endgame scenarios. First, a negotiated settlement among all parties. In February 2016 a ceasefire went into effect. About two weeks later, a new round of negotiations among the internal and foreign stakeholders began in Geneva. The Higher Negotiations Committee (HNC) spoke for the opposition. The HNC was made up of groups vetted by Saudi Arabia (a case of the fox guarding the chicken coop), groups selected from lists drawn up by Russia and Egypt, and a representative of the SNC. Neither ISIS nor Jabhat al-Nusra was included in either the ceasefire or the negotiations. Nor were representatives from any Kurdish group invited to Geneva, at Turkey's insistence.

After desultory negotiations, in which the opposition and the Syrian government refused to talk to each other directly, the opposition, citing ceasefire violations by the government, withdrew. The Syrian government and its Russian backers claimed they were targeting terrorist groups only, not the groups represented at the talks. Given the entanglement of various groups on the battlefield, as well as the expansiveness with which the Syrian and Russian governments define terrorists, their claim was a plausible, if cynical, one. US Secretary of State John Kerry spent the next several months attempting to restore the ceasefire and restart the talks, in vain.

The breakdown of the ceasefire wasn't the only challenge the talks faced. There were at least three others. First, after the Russian intervention in 2015, there was no incentive for the Syrian government and its Russian backer to negotiate in good faith. Both continued their military campaign. They did this either because they thought they could defeat the opposition outright, or because they thought that the more territory they had under their control, the better their bargaining position in any future talks. And given the government's existing battlefield gains, were it to enter into talks in the future it would do so only with the intention of negotiating the opposition's terms of surrender. There was also no incentive for those groups not invited to the talks, particularly ISIS and Jabhat al-Nusra, to abide by the ceasefire or, for that matter, any negotiated settlement. Indeed, it is in their interest to play the role of spoiler. Finally, the Saudi-Iranian proxy war discourages both states from reaching a compromise over Syria.

These problems are not unique to negotiations past; they are likely to plague any ceasefire-to-negotiations effort for the foreseeable future.

Since the chances of reaching a negotiated settlement are low, the likeliest scenario is what former UN and Arab League mediator, Lakhdar Brahimi, called the "Somalization" of Syria. As in the case of Somalia, Syria would have a single government which would reign, but not rule, over the entirety of its territory. It would have a permanent representative to the United Nations, issue passports and postage stamps, and even, if it so desired, send a team to the Olympics. As in the case of Somalia, armed militias would control large swathes of territory outside the control of the government. Since there would be no established boundaries between the territories, they would engage in perpetual warfare against one another or, at best, sign on to impermanent informal truces. In other words, the world would inherit one more failed state.

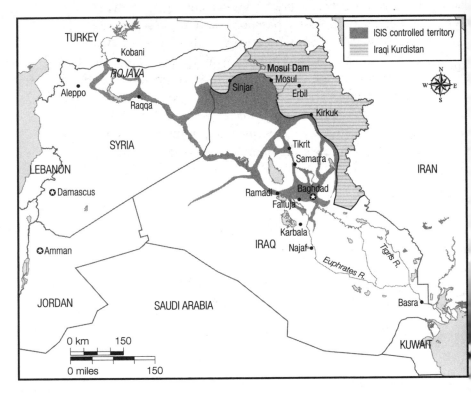

Map 3 Farthest expansion of the Islamic State in Syria and Iraq (2014)

4

THE RISE AND DECLINE OF ISIS

What is ISIS?

ISIS—also known as the Islamic State, ISIL, and Daesh—is a group committed to salafi principles and jihadi tactics. It is extremely brutal. The group has regularly beheaded and crucified those it considers its enemies, killed other Muslims for the crime of apostasy (leaving the fold), and committed acts of genocide against those it considers polytheists. In summer 2014, it conquered a broad swath of territory stretching from north/central Syria through central Iraq. The territory included the third largest city in Iraq, Mosul. A year later, it began a global campaign of terrorist attacks.

"ISIS"—which stands for the Islamic State of Iraq and Syria—is the most common term used to identify the group. Most policy makers and commentators shun the term "Islamic State" because it lends credence to ISIS's pretension to be recognized as a territorial state. The most common term in the Arab world is "Daesh," an Arabic acronym for *al-Dawla al-Islamiya fi al-'Iraq wal-Sham* that has the same meaning as ISIS. During the Obama administration, the official American term for the group was ISIL, which stands for the Islamic State of Iraq and the Levant. While unfamiliar, the term "Levant" is more accurate than the term "Syria." The word *Sham* in the original Arabic refers to a geographic unit larger than just the state of Syria (which, in

Arabic, is *Suriya*). Instead, it refers to "Greater Syria"—the territory that is currently Syria, Lebanon, Israel/Palestine, Jordan, and western Iraq. The term is an old one, coined by the French because the territory lies in the eastern Arab world (that is, not North Africa), where the sun rises (*se lève*).

Where did ISIS come from?

There are two wings of the leadership of ISIS, a political/ideological wing and a military wing. The first wing can be traced back to the Soviet invasion of Afghanistan in 1979, the second to the American invasion of Iraq in 2003.

The Soviet Union invaded Afghanistan in 1979, ostensibly at the request of an allied Afghan government which was facing a mounting insurgency. It remained there for ten years. During that time, jihadis (known as *mujahidin*, an equivalent term) from around the world flocked to Afghanistan to fight the invaders. They received financial and material assistance from the United States and Saudi Arabia. Among those jihadis was Osama bin Laden, the founder of al-Qaeda.

In 1989, another jihadi, Abu Musab al-Zarqawi, showed up in Afghanistan. As his name connotes, al-Zarqawi hailed from Zarqa, the third largest city in Jordan. In his youth, al-Zarqawi was a bootlegger, drunk, brawler, and, perhaps, pimp and sexual trafficker who had spent time in prison. A short while after his visit to Afghanistan, al-Zarqawi returned to Jordan where he was again arrested, this time for plotting to overthrow the government. He remained in prison until 1999, when King Hussein of Jordan died and his son, Prince Abdullah, took the throne. As was customary, Abdullah celebrated his accession by declaring a general amnesty. Released, al-Zarqawi returned to Afghanistan.

After his return, al-Zarqawi met with bin Laden, who, accounts tell us, was not terribly impressed. Nevertheless, bin Laden gave Zarqawi a seed grant to set up a training camp for Jordanian and Palestinian jihadis there, and to establish his own organization, al-Tawhid wal-Jihad (*tawhid* refers to the oneness and dominion of God, the fundamental principle of Islam). After 9/11 and the American invasion of Afghanistan in 2001, al-Zarqawi fled, first to Iran, then to Iraq. When Americans invaded Iraq, al-Tawhid wal-Jihad became al-Qaeda in Iraq and al-Zarqawi undertook a terrorist campaign. This campaign was unlike the campaigns waged by other insurgents: Instead of targeting the invaders alone, al-Qaeda in Iraq targeted Shi'is as well, something al-Qaeda Central (that is, al-Qaeda in Afghanistan and Pakistan) had never done and, in fact, warned against.

The Americans killed al-Zarqawi in an airstrike in 2006. After his death, al-Qaeda in Iraq went through several permutations under various leaders, none of whom died peacefully in his bed. One of those groups was the Islamic State of Iraq, and one of those leaders (whether he was the second or third is disputed) was Abu Bakr al-Baghdadi, now leader of the Islamic State.

Although his name suggests he was born in Baghdad, Abu Bakr al-Baghdadi was born in Samarra, Iraq, in 1971. He received a higher religious education in Baghdad. He was either radicalized when he was interned at an American prison in Iraq, Camp Bucca, or when he met al-Zarqawi. After becoming leader of the Islamic State of Iraq, he permitted Syrian-born fighters in it to return to Syria. While they soon split with al-Baghdadi's group, al-Baghdadi rechristened his organization the "Islamic State of Iraq and Syria"—ISIS. He and his cohort form the inner circle of the political/ideological wing of ISIS's leadership.

The military wing of ISIS's leadership consists of former Iraqi military officers who had served under Iraq's pre-invasion president, Saddam Hussein. Like Saddam, they came overwhelmingly from the minority Sunni population of Iraq. After the American invasion, the American pro-consul, Paul Bremer, issued two controversial orders ("pro-consul" is roughly the same as colonial administrator). Coalition

Provisional Authority (CPA) Order No. 1 dissolved the ruling party of Iraq, the Baath Party, to which high-ranking military officers belonged (separate Baath parties ruled both Syria and Iraq). CPA Order No. 2 dissolved the army. Unfortunately for the Americans, no one thought to disarm the army before dissolving it. In effect, the Americans loosed large numbers of unemployed, armed youths and their military leaders upon the population of Iraq. A group of those leaders went underground. Some analysts argue that this was the plan all along. They claim that Saddam, realizing his army could not stand up to the American army, ordered his generals to set up military networks that would harass the Americans after the invasion.

That which brought those military officers together with the political/ideological wing of ISIS was a common hatred of the Shi'i-dominated Iraqi government the Americans installed. By 2012, that government was waging a violent campaign against its Sunni opposition. The officers organized resistance to the government, then engineered ISIS's takeover of a tract of territory in Syria and Iraq the size of Belgium, as the cliché has it. As of August 2015, there were reportedly one hundred to 160 former officers in positions of command in Iraq. Seven of the twelve governors in ISIS-held Iraqi territory were former officers as well.

What does ISIS believe?

Osama bin Laden and Abu Musab al-Zarqawi both cut their teeth waging jihad in Afghanistan, and al-Qaeda in Iraq was an affiliate of al-Qaeda Central. Nevertheless, the two were very different organizations. As a matter of fact, al-Qaeda Central was always wary of its affiliate. Even before the well-known hostility erupted into the open, al-Qaeda Central chided its obstreperous spawn publically for transforming a war against the American "Crusaders" in Iraq into a war against Shi'is there.

The hostility between the two organizations is partly rooted in their competition for leadership of the global jihadi movement.

But it is also rooted in competing ideologies. Although most Islamist organizations founded during the 1980s and 1990s fought against the regimes in their home states, from its inception al-Qaeda operated differently. Instead of fighting the "near enemy" (that is, local rulers), al-Qaeda believes in fighting the far enemy that makes up the "Crusader-Zionist Conspiracy." The conspiracy consists of all those who have warred on Muslims. This includes not just the United States and Israel, but also Russia (which has waged war in Chechnya), China (which represses its Uighur population), India (which claims predominantly Muslim Kashmir), and others. According to al-Qaeda, this conspiracy was responsible for carving up the Islamic world into numerous nation-states to keep it weak and divided.

The strategy of al-Qaeda has been to "vex and exhaust" members of the conspiracy by goading them into debilitating adventures abroad where al-Qaeda can bleed them. The group derived its strategy from its experience in Afghanistan where, it claims, its attacks against the Soviet military led directly to the collapse of the Soviet Union. It was the reason al-Qaeda welcomed the American invasion and occupation of Iraq. It is still al-Qaeda's strategy. Hence, its provocative terrorist acts abroad.

The strategy of ISIS is quite different. ISIS has sought to seize territory and purify it from foreign influences and from those it considers "unIslamic"—Yazidi Kurds, secular Kurds, Shiʻis, and the like. Overall, ISIS's strategic vision can be reduced to three words: *khilafa*, *takfir*, and *hijra*.

Khilafa means "caliphate" in Arabic. According to al-Baghdadi and his followers, Islam requires a caliphate—that is, a territory in which Muslims might practice true Islam. A caliph (*khalifa*—literally, successor [to Muhammad]) is the individual who rules over the caliphate. His role is to protect Islam and defend and expand the territory of the caliphate. Traditionally, to be a caliph a Muslim has to fulfill a number of requirements, including piety, religious knowledge, and descent from the family of the prophet. When his forces seized Mosul in summer

2014, al-Baghdadi proclaimed himself caliph. He burnished his credentials for the job by adopting the title and changing his name to Caliph Ibrahim (his original first name) al-Qurayshi al-Hashimi. The latter two names signify that he is a member of the tribe of Muhammad (al-Quraysh) and a descendant of the prophet.

The second keyword is *takfir*, which refers to the act of pronouncing Muslims who disagree with ISIS's strict interpretation of Islamic Law to be apostates, a crime punishable by death. This is the reason for ISIS's murderous rampages against Shi'is—rampages that even al-Qaeda central has found counterproductive, if not repugnant. Resurrecting the concept of *takfir* was the brainchild of Abu Musab al-Zarqawi. His strategy was to spark tit-for-tat violence between Sunnis and Shi'is in Iraq. By doing this, he hoped to mobilize the Sunni community and make Iraq ungovernable for the Americans. Al-Baghdadi has gone one step further than al-Zarqawi. He finds the concept useful in his effort to purify the territory of the caliphate which, he believes, will soon stretch wherever Muslims rule or have ruled in the past.

The final word is *hijra*, the migration of Muslims from *dar al-harb* (the abode of war; that is, non-Muslim-majority countries) to *dar al-Islam* (the abode of Islam). The model for this is Muhammad and his early companions, who migrated from Mecca, where they had been persecuted, to Medina, where they established the first permanent Islamic community. ISIS wants a great incoming of Muslims into the caliphate, both because it needs skilled administrators and fighters and because it considers emigration from "non-Muslim territory" to "Muslim territory" a religious obligation.

Is ISIS apocalyptic?

According to some commentators, there is a fourth idea al-Baghdadi brought to the table: an apocalyptic vision. They claim that members of ISIS believe that the end of days is near, a time when righteousness will achieve its final victory over disbelief. They base their claim on ISIS's own propaganda, particularly the name of ISIS's glossy magazine, *Dabiq*. Dabiq is a site in northern Syria where, according to Islamic lore, a great battle will be fought between ISIS and "Rome" (*Rum* in Arabic refers to the Christian West). This battle will set in motion a cascade of events that will eventually bring about the reign of justice and virtue.

It's not too much of a stretch to attribute an apocalyptic vision to ISIS. All monotheistic religions are prone to apocalyptic visions. It is a logical explanation for the presence of evil and those who do not believe as you do in spite of the existence of an all-powerful God. At some point, He must surely act to make things right.

There are, however, reasons for skepticism. Whatever the future may hold, ISIS, like some apocalyptic Christian groups, has in the meantime proved itself so tactically and strategically adept that it has obviously kicked any end-of-days can well down the road. Further, the idea that ISIS has an apocalyptic vision discounts the importance of the military wing of ISIS's leadership. If hard-headed former Iraqi Baath military officers think about an apocalypse at all, they probably treat it much as Hitler's generals treated the musings of Nazi true believers—with a roll of their eyes. And if any of the principals from the political/ideological wing of the leadership were to propose acting in a way that might jeopardize the former officers' dream of ruling over a liberated Sunni state in the heart of the Arab world, those officers might just get rid of their former comrades in arms.

According to one author who has bought into the whole ISIS/apocalypse idea, "For certain true believers—the kind who long for epic good-versus-evil battles—visions of apocalyptic bloodbaths fulfill a deep psychological need."[1] Or, perhaps, playing up a purported ISIS/apocalypse link fulfils a deep psychological need for those who just cannot otherwise account for the savagery and fervor of ISIS devotees. Foregrounding ISIS's apocalyptic worldview enables us to disparage the group as irrational and even medieval. If the recent past has demonstrated one thing, it is that ISIS thrives when its adversaries underestimate it.

ISIS conquered the town of Dabiq in August 2014. Turkish-backed rebel forces retook it in October 2016. According to reports, ISIS fighters in the town put up minimal resistance, and before the final assault many stole off into the night.

Is ISIS "Islamic"?

In September 2014, shortly after the United States launched military operations against ISIS, Barack Obama opined, "ISIL is not Islamic." "No religion condones the killing of innocents," he continued, "and the vast majority of ISIL's victims have been Muslim."[2] Obama's statement is troublesome on two counts. First, by deciding just what is and what is not Islamic, Obama appears to have been engaging in his own brand of *takfir* (as did Pope Francis when he stated that Donald Trump "was not Christian"). Second, for someone outside a religious tradition to pass judgment on what does or does not belong to that tradition is just plain presumptuous.

Simply put, ISIS is an instance of a phenomenon that recurs in most religions, and certainly in all monotheistic religions. Every so often militant strains emerge, flourish temporarily, then usually vanish. They are then replaced by another militant strain whose own beginning is linked to a predecessor by nothing more profound than drawing from the same cultural pool as its predecessor.

In the seventh century there were the Kharajites (the first sect of Islam), a starkly puritanical group that assassinated two of the early caliphs. Like ISIS, the Kharajites thought they knew best what and who were truly Islamic, and what and who were not.

In the eighteenth century there were the followers of Muhammad ibn ʿAbd al-Wahhab, a central Arabian preacher whose devotees included Muhammad ibn Saud, the founder of the Saudi dynasty. ʿAbd al-Wahhab believed that the worship of saints and the construction of mausoleums were impious acts. As a result, ibn Saud's army destroyed sites holy to both Sunnis and Shi'is in Arabia and present-day Iraq, much as ISIS targets sites from antiquity today.

During the nineteenth century, Muhammad Ahmad, a member of a religious order in what is now Sudan, proclaimed himself *mahdi* (redeemer of the Islamic faith), just as Abu Bakr al-Baghdadi proclaimed himself caliph—a more prosaic position. Ahmad's army overran Khartoum, where it massacred a British-led garrison and beheaded its commander.

From time to time (it is impossible to predict when), some figure emerges in each monotheistic tradition who puts his own spin on that tradition. To be successful, that spin must capture the imagination of some of that tradition's adherents, who then try to put it into practice. Some spins, such as that of contemporary Saudi Arabia's Wahhabis, have sticking power. This is not because they are somehow "truer" than others, but because those who advocate for them are better able to mobilize resources—a core group of committed followers, military capabilities, outside support, oil revenue—than others. Most do not. Considering what it is up against and its own shortcomings, ISIS will probably fall into the latter category.

Why was ISIS able to conquer so much territory so quickly?

ISIS began its conquests in January 2014, when it took Raqqa, a provincial capital in Syria. The city had been the first to fall to opposition forces led by Jabhat al-Nusra, Ahrar al-Sham, and the Free Syrian Army. Immediately after the conquest, ISIS established a civil administration. An article in the first issue of *Dabiq* describes these and ensuing events:

Then the events of Sham began to unfold and the Islamic State quickly got involved, answering the cries of the weak and oppressed Muslims by sending a mission from Iraq to activate its units in Sham and later make the announcement of its official expansion.

Again, pride, envy, nationalism, and innovation led to events similar to those of Iraq. New sahwat [foreign-supported opposition forces, such as those that aided American forces against the insurgency in Iraq] were formed with the exact same financial, political, and "scholarly" support [quotation marks in original]. They repeated the mistakes of their predecessors in Iraq and decided to enter into war with the Islamic State, but here Allah blessed the mujahidin in a manner unique to the lands of Sham, so that quickly Sahwah treachery was exposed and destroyed. Then, by Allah's grace, the mujahidin gained control over territory larger than many states claiming "legality" today, lands formerly under control of the Umawi khulafa' [the first Islamic dynasty] of Sham and the 'Abbasi khulafa' [the second Islamic dynasty] of Iraq.

Thereafter, the hopes of the khulafa' became an undeniable reality, one that allowed no room for anyone claiming any excuse to resist authority of the imam except to be dealt with by the decisive law of Allah. The victories in Ninawa, al-Anbar, Salahuddin, al-Khayr, al-Barakah, and elsewhere all aided the declaration made by the Islamic State on the first day of Ramadan 1435 [according to the Islamic calendar], in which the Khilafah was officially announced.[3]

The ISIS offensive lasted six months and involved only about 2,000 ISIS fighters. Little wonder, then, that the breathless *Dabiq* article attributes the victory to divine plan.

With all due respect for the Author of that plan, more prosaic factors contributed to ISIS's victory. First, while the tactical and strategic capabilities of the military wing of ISIS were hardly a match for the American-led coalition which invaded Iraq in 2003, it was more than adequate to take on the new foe—the Iraqi army. The Islamic State is unlike many earlier groups that have arisen in Islamic history around some charismatic leader, only to be defeated because it had no understanding of warfare.

The second reason for ISIS's success was that it played to the grievances in Sunni-dominated regions of Iraq against the American-imposed Shi'i government in Baghdad. Sunnis directed their anger in particular at Iraqi prime minister Nouri al-Maliki, a Shi'i politician whose spitefulness was matched only by his ineptitude. ISIS exploited Sunni anger, calling on Sunnis to take up arms against the government. Whatever the efficacy of ISIS's call, Sunni grievances ran deep.

Perhaps the most important reason for the success of ISIS's campaign was the collapse of the Iraqi army. ISIS did not win its territory; the Iraqi army lost it. Iraqi soldiers threw down their weapons and ran.

Military analysts give a number of reasons for the collapse. First, after the Americans disbanded the Iraqi army in 2003, they had to build a new one from scratch. Its structure was based on the American model, which might not have been suitable for Iraqi needs. Second, like most armies in the Arab world, the Iraqi army was designed for use against internal opposition and not to defeat an armed foe invading from the outside. Finally, analysts attribute the collapse of the army to the increasing sectarianization and corruption of the Iraqi regime under Nouri al-Maliki. The government considered positions of command a form of political patronage. Sectarian identity, family background, and loyalty to the prime minister counted more for appointment and promotion than training or ability.

In the end, many Iraqi Sunnis saw the army as an institution designed to maintain Shi'i political dominance, not as an impartial national institution, and refused to enlist in it. Many Sunnis feared that the army would retaliate against them for "collaborating" with ISIS or simply out of spite. Given a choice between the army and ISIS, some chose the latter. Others simply fled. Acts of violence committed by the Shi'i militias participating in the government's counteroffensive against ISIS have all too often demonstrated how well grounded their fear was.

Who joins ISIS?

ISIS recruits both from within the territory under its control and neighboring areas, and from abroad. According to Radio Free Europe/Radio Liberty,[4] as of 2013—that is, before ISIS's major push—there were between 17,000 and 19,000 ISIS members in Iraq and Syria. This is probably a low-ball estimate. As of 2015, there were about 30,000, more than enough to replace the 15,000 killed by the American-led bombing campaign during the first year of that campaign. A majority came from the Middle East. The largest number of Arabs who hail from places other than Iraq and Syria came from Saudi Arabia and Tunisia. Other fighters came from as far away as North America, Europe (Belgium has supplied the largest per capita contingent from Europe), Australia, and the Caucasus (particularly Chechnya). Most Europeans who have joined ISIS are Muslim immigrants or the descendants of Muslim immigrants.

Social scientists cite a number of reasons people join ISIS. Some of those recruited in Iraq and Syria, they assert, join because they believe in ISIS's message. Others, however, join because they are compelled by ISIS to do so, or for revenge, money, sectarian sentiments, camaraderie, or the promise of power or sex slaves (ISIS sells its members captured Yazidi women and girls). Other social scientists claim that the sense of empowerment that comes from joining a group noted for its ultra-violence, disaffection from society, and just plain sociopathy might also factor into the calculations of European Muslims who face discrimination and impoverishment in their adopted homes. Then there is bloodlust, the promise of adventure, the lure of joining the baddest gang in town, and thrill seeking. The list is so long that one is reminded of something the late US Supreme Court Justice Antonin Scalia once said: "[I]nterior decorating is a rock hard science compared to psychology practiced by amateurs."[5]

Many ISIS attacks around the globe are carried out by individuals the media have dubbed "lone wolves"—that is, freelancers who act without the direct knowledge of the ISIS leadership (to avoid glamorizing them, the RAND Corporation prefers the term "flaming bananas".[6]) There are two theories why these individuals—or, indeed, those who travel to the caliphate to join ISIS—pledge allegiance to the group. The first is that they get "radicalized." Radicalization refers to a step-by-step process whereby individuals become increasingly susceptible to jihadi ideas. First, they cut themselves off from social networks such as family, which provide them with support and a conventional value system. They then immerse themselves in a radical counterculture. They might do this on their own, or a jihadi recruiter might bring them into the fold. Either way, the result is the same.

Most attempts to counter ISIS base their efforts on this model. For example, the US Department of State has released a short video titled, "Run—Don't Walk—to ISIS Land." The video shows graphic images of crucifixions, beheadings, suicide bombings, and the destruction of mosques perpetrated by ISIS members. It ends with a warning: "Think again—turn away."[7] Interestingly, the video mimics ISIS propaganda, which, some observers claim, plays a key role in recruitment. Rather than presenting a religious rationale for ISIS's actions, the group's propaganda tends to shun a religious pitch. Instead, it focuses on the violence the group perpetrates. ISIS has even released a video game based on Grand Theft Auto. Rather than stealing cars and battling the police, the player destroys advancing personnel carriers and shoots enemy soldiers.[8] This being the case, perhaps the radicalization model is wrong or not universally applicable.

There is other evidence that it is wrong as well. For example, there is the widely reported story of two would-be jihadists who, before they left Birmingham, UK, for Syria, ordered

Islam for Dummies and *The Koran for Dummies* to fill the gaps in their knowledge. Newspaper stories time and again puzzle over the problem of how it happens that individuals who go on to join ISIS were found in bars (sometimes gay bars), or had Western girlfriends, or smoked and drank almost up to the time they committed some act of violence for the group (the most common explanation: their dissolute lifestyle was a cover). And after the driver of a truck ran down and killed eighty-four people in Nice, France, the French interior minister was at a loss to explain how someone who drank during Ramadan (which had ended a week and a half before) could have radicalized so quickly.

A number of experts have thus argued that the radicalization model should be replaced by or supplemented with a different model. Rather than joining a radically different religious counterculture, they argue that individuals are attracted to ISIS because its actions reaffirm the cultural values of those who are marginalized or those who exhibit what psychiatrists call "social personality disorders." Is it really all that difficult to understand how ISIS volunteers might be drawn to a value system that asserts an aggressive machismo, disparages steady work, and sustains the impulse for immediate gratification—a value system that promotes redemption through violence, loyalty, patriarchal values, self-sacrifice to the point of martyrdom, and the diminution of women to objects of pleasure? In this reading, ISIS more closely resembles the sort of street gang with which many of its Western and Westernized enlistees are familiar than its more austere competitor, al-Qaeda.

Where has ISIS spread?

After its rapid-fire conquests in Syria and Iraq during 2014, ISIS seemed to run out of steam. With the exception of Palmyra, Syria, which ISIS took during spring 2015, ISIS captured few significant prizes on the battlefield. In fact, ISIS-held territory began to contract. By spring 2016 American military analysts estimated that ISIS had lost 45 percent of its territory in Iraq and 20 percent in Syria. ISIS faced the Syrian army in the northwest and west, Kurdish forces and Turkey in the north, and Shiʻi-dominated territory in the east and southeast. It had reached the farthest extent of its expansion in Syria and Iraq. By that time, however, ISIS had already cast its eye elsewhere.

ISIS set up shop outside Iraq and Syria. Groups of militants in Africa and Asia have pledged allegiance to ISIS and have established what ISIS calls "wilayat" (provinces; singular: wilaya) outside the borders of the caliphate. Sometimes those groups were preexisting. Sometimes they were deliberately spawned by ISIS. And sometimes they were founded by independents or ISIS members who had cut their teeth in the caliphate. ISIS believes that over time there will be enough of these provinces and they will expand to such an extent that they will naturally flow into one another, forming one large caliphate. One analyst has called this the "ink spot strategy"[9] (not to be confused with the "lily pad strategy" adopted by the US military to defeat ISIS in Iraq). In addition to gaining stature through their association with ISIS, affiliates frequently receive direct assistance in the form of advisers and fighters from ISIS in Syria and Iraq.

ISIS affiliates thrive in places that lack effective governance. One of the largest (upwards of 6,000 members in 2016) and most successful was established in Libya. Taking advantage of the anarchic conditions that followed the ouster of Muammar Qaddafi, it seized control over the coastal city of Sirte and the surrounding area. It also established a presence in Benghazi. By the beginning of 2016, ISIS claimed affiliates not only in Libya, but in Algeria, the Sinai Peninsula of Egypt, Saudi Arabia, Yemen, the Caucasus, Afghanistan/Pakistan, and Nigeria. The Nigerian wilaya came about when Boko Haram—a salafi/jihadi group responsible for about 20,000 deaths in West Africa—pledged allegiance to the caliphate. In Boko Haram, ISIS met its match in brutality.

What is life in the Islamic State like?

At its height, ISIS ruled from five million to six million people. Most of them lived in the cities of Syria and Iraq, including Raqqa and Palmyra in Syria, and Mosul, Fallujah, Ramadi, and Tikrit in Iraq. There has been a lot of unnecessary debate over whether ISIS actually controlled the entire territory or whether it controlled only the cities that were linked by a network of roads. Of course it controlled it: Just because there are no post boxes in the wilds of Alaska does not mean that people who live there don't know they should pay their taxes.

As part of the process of conquest, ISIS sought to "purify" the territory it was taking over. This meant putting to flight or killing "apostates" such as Shiʻis, secular Kurds, and "polytheists" such as Yazidis. When ISIS took over Mosul, 30,000 Mosuli Christians fled. ISIS has been particularly brutal to the Yazidis, however. During its conquest of Sinjar in northwest Iraq, ISIS fighters slaughtered between 2,000 and 5,000 Yazidi men, sold more than 3,000 Yazidi women and girls into slavery, and drove about 50,000 Yazidis into the mountains where they faced starvation and dehydration. Kurdish forces, backed up by American airpower, eventually lifted the ISIS siege of their mountain redoubt. Yazidis are endogamous; that is, they permit marriage only within the Yazidi community. At the time of the abductions, Yazidis considered marriage or sexual relations outside the community a crime punishable by death. The enslavement of Yazidi women by ISIS therefore would have been tantamount to genocide had not the Yazidi religious authority, Baba Sheikh, called on the community to treat its victimized sisters with compassion soon after the first abductees began returning.

ISIS's caliphate looks and functions like a normal state—a particularly vicious one, it is true, but a state nonetheless. It has issued license plates and building permits, has a court and educational system, and attempted (but ultimately failed) to issue its own currency (it now accepts only infidel US dollars for tax, water, and electricity payments). It even has a flag and a national anthem, which citizens of the caliphate must sing a capella to comply with ISIS's ban on musical instruments. And like all other states the caliphate has taken on both disciplinary and service functions. ISIS is far better at the former than the latter.

ISIS runs its caliphate according to its interpretation of Islamic law, which, for ISIS, covers all aspects of people's lives, public and private (according to ISIS, the two separate domains do not exist in Islam). Its purview runs the gamut from diet and gender relations to mandatory prayers and charity (local officials collect and redistribute money for alms). Alcohol and public smoking are prohibited. According to the ISIS legal code, the penalty for drinking and smoking is eighty lashes, although repeat offenders face execution. Dress is strictly regulated. Women must cover themselves; men must wear beards. The only men women can mix with in public are their husbands or immediate family members. Makeup for girls is prohibited, as are jeans. The penalty for engaging in homosexual acts is death; those caught are commonly thrown off buildings. Shops must close during prayers. And the list goes on. ISIS has its own police force-cum-vice squad called the *hisba* (Arabic for "accountability") to enforce the rules.

One telling anecdote displays how the population in ISIS-controlled territory has reacted to the beheadings, crucifixions, amputations, and stonings to which the group regularly condemns those convicted of "crimes." After ISIS began displaying severed heads on a fence surrounding Naeem ("Heaven") Park in Raqqa, the inhabitants of the city began referring to it as Jahim Park. "Jahim" means Hell in Arabic.

After the conquests of 2014, ISIS divided the territory of Syria and Iraq into nineteen wilayat, each with its own military and administrative branches. Each wilaya oversees ISIS-run courts, prisons, and schools. Children receive mandatory instruction in the Qur'an, for which parents must pay. ISIS also sponsors shari'a (Islamic law) camps for boys under fifteen and military camps for those over that age. In addition, in each wilaya an administrative unit called *diwan al-khidamat,* or "services bureau," tends to the needs of the inhabitants of the province, at least in theory. There is, however, a catch: ISIS does not provide its services for free. Those living in cities, for example, must pay for their garbage collection and drinkable water as an add-on. Life in ISIS-controlled Syria and Iraq means being subject to ISIS's extortionate practices at virtually every turn.

Because ISIS has not attracted into the caliphate the skilled administrators and technicians it needs to run hospitals, electrical grids, sanitation facilities, and water treatment plants, and because so many administrators and technicians already living there fled ISIS rule, urban conditions have deteriorated. A year after ISIS took over Mosul, the administration of the city ran out of chlorine. As a result, water became undrinkable. Diseases like hepatitis spread and essentials like flour were in short supply. The experience in Raqqa was similar. A year after the city came under ISIS control, water and electricity were available for no more than three or four hours a day, and garbage rotted in the streets. The problem of keeping skilled civil servants went from bad to worse after the Syrian and Iraqi governments stopped paying the salaries of their employees who worked in ISIS-controlled areas. There was only one incentive for them to stay: If they were caught leaving without permission, ISIS would execute them.

Running a state, even badly, requires money. In the beginning, ISIS financed itself much as al-Qaeda had—from donations, mainly from the Gulf. After its conquests in 2014, it could tap other sources of revenue. These included the one-time infusion of cash from looted banks, oil (which it refined and smuggled out, mainly to Turkey), ransoms from kidnapped locals and foreigners, and the sale of artifacts (Palmyra and Nineveh offered a particularly rich cache). ISIS also relied on internal revenue streams, such as a poll tax on Christians (called *jizya*) and other taxes, the sale of services, confiscations, and extortion. ISIS taxes practically everything, from income

(10 percent) to a $1,000 departure tax to all who receive per-mission to leave. ISIS also controlled one-third of Iraq's wheat and barley crop and took over a phosphate mine, phosphate and sulfur plants, and cement-making facilities, from which it derived more than $1 billion a year.

Over time, many of these sources dried up: international banking regulations made the transfer of money from donors difficult, there were fewer opportunities for kidnappings, and global and domestic law enforcement agencies cracked down on the trade in looted artifacts. Revenue from oil plummeted, not only because the price of oil hit a thirteen-year low, but because Turkey tightened its border and American aircraft tar-geted mobile oil refineries and tanker trucks. This made rev-enue streams that came from the populations ISIS ruled all the more important.

By 2016, experts working in the US Department of the Treasury and other agencies estimated that about 50 percent of ISIS's revenue came from confiscations and taxation. This was followed by revenue from the sale of oil (estimated to con-tribute about 43 percent of ISIS's income). The remainder came from kidnappings, drug smuggling, donations, and the sale of services and artifacts. ISIS's dependence on revenue from confiscations and taxation is not a sustainable revenue model. With little being produced and exports diminished, ISIS is overly dependent on non-replenishable resources. And it is eating its own seed corn.

Why did the United States undertake military action against ISIS?

On August 7, 2014, President Barack Obama announced that he was authorizing both military and humanitarian missions in Iraq. In a way, this was not surprising: The president had announced two months earlier that he had tasked the National Security Council to prepare a list of American options as ISIS was advancing there. In his August speech, Obama cited two reasons for his actions. First, ISIS was threatening the Iraqi city of Erbil, where US diplomats and military personnel were stationed. Second, American airstrikes were necessary to break the ISIS siege of Sinjar, and airdrops of food and water to beleaguered Yazidis there would prevent a humanitarian disaster.

The initial strategy was to relieve the immediate danger, then contain ISIS and slowly push it back. When ISIS launched its global campaign of terror and Americans and others demanded a stronger response, that strategy became politically unfeasible. The United States ramped up its involvement. It closely coordinated its efforts with the main Kurdish groups operating in Syria and Iraq, the Peoples' Protection Units (YPG) and the Peshmerga (fighters from Iraqi Kurdistan), sometimes embedding Special Forces in their units. It also assembled an independent anti-ISIS militia, the Syrian Democratic Forces, made up predominantly of units from the YPG but including Arab members of the Free Syrian Army and other forces. The hope was that establishing a mixed force would make the liberation of towns appear to be a united Syrian affair, not just the work of Kurds. It was also hoped that a mixed force would prevent the ethnic cleansing of Arabs from predominantly Kurdish areas. That hope was all too often dashed.

Looking at it in another way, however, Obama's action is surprising. Obama had never been a big fan of humanitarian intervention, and the disaster in Libya undoubtedly confirmed his reservations. He had opposed the war in Iraq in 2003 and by the time he took office the war had become deeply unpopular. Obama had overseen the withdrawal of the last US troops during his first term and was reluctant to get drawn into another. Furthermore, before ISIS's final thrust through Iraq in summer 2014, Obama had disparaged ISIS, famously comparing it to a J.V. (junior varsity) team for al-Qaeda in remarks six months earlier.[10] Launching an offensive against the group was quite an about-face. Finally, ISIS had yet to strike the United States or inspire others to do so. It first drew US blood after the US air campaign against it had begun, when it brutally executed two American journalists. At the time, its focus was purely local.

Over time, the administration added those executions, the need to protect the Mosul Dam, and other reasons to justify and expand the campaign. The United States recruited other countries into the effort as well. By the beginning of 2016, their aircraft had flown close to 2,000 sorties. So, what is the real story behind the air campaign, the arming of Kurdish groups fighting ISIS, and the deployment of Special Forces and military advisers?

The answer may lie in an analogy Obama made to advisers, apparently on more than one occasion. As recounted in *The Atlantic*, the president used the 2008 Batman movie, *The Dark Knight*, to explain the need for direct American involvement. "There's a scene in the beginning in which the gang leaders of Gotham are meeting," Obama said.

> These are men who had the city divided up. They were thugs, but there was a kind of order. Everyone had his turf. And then the Joker comes in and lights the whole city on fire. ISIL is the Joker. It has the capacity to set the whole region on fire. That's why we have to fight it.[11]

In other words, by uniting Syria and Iraq in a caliphate, and by threatening their neighbors, ISIS was on the verge of redrawing the map of the region. The United States was once again intervening in the Middle East to preserve the state system there.

Why did ISIS begin its global campaign of terrorist attacks?

On November 13, 2015, suicide bombers and gunmen launched coordinated attacks in Paris. Three suicide bombers blew themselves up near a soccer stadium, killing themselves and four bystanders. The death toll would have been higher had there not been heightened security at the entrances to the stadium—a result of the presence of the president of France at the match between France and Germany. Simultaneously, gunmen fanned out throughout the city, opening fire with assault rifles and throwing grenades. Another suicide bomber blew himself up in a café after placing an order; fifteen customers were injured. The worst violence took place in the Bataclan Theater, which was packed with concertgoers listening to an American rock band. There, gunmen once again opened fire and threw grenades. They also took hostages, whom they threatened to behead. By the time police assaulted and entered the theater, eighty-nine concertgoers lay dead. ISIS claimed responsibility.

The attack in Paris was one of a series of attacks attributed to ISIS. Some, like that attack, were intricately planned. Others, like the attack in San Bernardino, California, were the work of individuals who had pledged allegiance to ISIS only a short time before. In all, from spring 2014, when the first attack attributed to ISIS occurred outside Syria and Iraq, through the 2016 attack in Nice, France, where a truck driver rammed into a crowd celebrating Bastille Day, close to 2,000 people died in attacks attributed to ISIS.

Although ISIS had called on supporters early on to attack military and police targets where those supporters lived, the wave of terrorism in Europe and the United States expanded dramatically after autumn 2015. That was when an ISIS affiliate in the Sinai, Egypt, claimed credit for setting off a bomb on a Russian airliner, killing 224. But that was also a year after ISIS had established its caliphate. What was the point of attacking foreigners in their home countries when retribution was sure to come and the location of the group that claimed responsibility was well known?

Setting aside the fact that ISIS at its highest levels might not have ordered all the attacks, and setting aside the fact that no one knows for sure how ISIS makes policy or even if it operates with a coherent strategic blueprint, it might be possible to venture a guess. Although many commentators have asserted that the ISIS attacks were a sign of the organization's global reach, it is more likely that the attacks signal the organization's increasing weakness and vulnerability.

There are a number of reasons to think this. First, in the lead-up to the escalation of attacks abroad, ISIS had been pushed back in both Iraq and Syria. Since ISIS's recruitment depends on its ability to demonstrate that it is the most brutally effective jihadi group in the world, the campaign may be ISIS's way of regaining prestige. In a similar vein, the attacks may have been aimed at reversing the *hijra* out of the territory of the Islamic State—another sign of ISIS failure. True, Syrians who joined the greatest refugee migration since the end of World War II were fleeing Syrian government violence as much as ISIS violence. Nevertheless, the attacks had the effect of reversing the initial sympathy Europeans and Americans had felt toward the refugees and led to demands for restricting their entrance.

There are two other arguments for believing that ISIS's shift in tactics is a sign of its lashing out like a cornered animal. First, the evolution of ISIS's tactics corresponds closely to the evolution of other territorially based jihadi groups that have been on the ropes. As al-Shabab, which operates in Somalia, lost ground to an international coalition, for example, it shifted to suicide operations and attacks in Kenya, Uganda, and Tanzania launched by fighters associated with the group. Boko Haram in West Africa did the same. Finally, why would any group change tactics if it thought it was winning?

What impact has ISIS had on the Middle East?

Although ISIS is a relatively recent phenomenon, the impact it has and will continue to have on the region is vast. In Syria, Iraq, Libya, and Yemen it has contributed to the weakening—perhaps beyond repair—of states and state institutions. In Tunisia it threatens the foundations of a fragile democratic transition, and in Egypt its presence is one of the excuses the regime uses to legitimize its harsh repression. The *takfiri* beliefs of ISIS have driven sectarianization in the territories in which it operates, and the spillover of that sectarianization has been felt region-wide. As villages and towns seesawed between ISIS and those fighting ISIS in Iraq, for example, murders of Sunnis by Shiʻi militias succeeded murders of Shiʻis at the hands of ISIS. The sectarianism ISIS has generated is thus unlikely to subside soon, if ever. A similar story might be told of the territory from which Kurds had fled, parts of which they cleansed of their Arab inhabitants upon their return.

ISIS was never a real threat to the nation-state system in the Middle East. There are too many stakeholders in the system for it to be. Hence, American intervention. Nevertheless, ISIS upset the balance of power among states in the region and exacerbated the not-necessarily cold war between Iran and Saudi Arabia. It has also exacerbated tensions between the United States and its partners, particularly Turkey and Saudi Arabia. The United States has viewed them as undercutting or even sabotaging its war on the group. ISIS has also drawn the United States and other states both inside and outside the region into yet another war in the Middle East.

ISIS has decimated ancient minority communities (as well as much of the region's ancient heritage) throughout the territory it has controlled or sought to control. Christians and Yazidis have fled its onslaught, and, in the case of Yazidis, have died or been enslaved in large numbers at its hands. Christians and Yazidis escaping ISIS territory have swelled the ranks of others fleeing the ISIS assault or the harshness of ISIS rule. In cities and towns where ISIS and anti-ISIS forces battle, civilians have been caught in the crossfire or have faced starvation or massacre. Even when ISIS is pushed back the violence continues, as neighbors seek to settle old scores and "collaborators" are punished for their betrayal. Just as noteworthy, in a region in which governments are no strangers to brutality, ISIS has set a new standard for politically motivated violence.

What does the future hold for the ISIS caliphate?

If 2014 was the year in which ISIS seemed unstoppable, 2015 was the year the ISIS caliphate began its slide into oblivion. In

January 2015, Kurdish YPG and Peshmerga forces retook the town of Kobani from ISIS. The town is important because it borders on Turkey. By capturing it, Kurdish forces, not ISIS, attained control of the border, impeding the smuggling of oil that was so vital for ISIS's economy. In addition, Kobani was key to ensuring the territorial continuity of Rojava. Its capture thus represented a milestone in fulfilling Kurdish ambitions for an autonomous or independent Kurdistan in northern Syria. At the end of March, Iraqi security forces and Shi'i militias, backed by coalition air power, retook the city of Tikrit, the birthplace of Saddam Hussein. Nine months later, Iraqi commandos, again backed by allied airpower, retook the city of Ramadi. In March 2016, Syrian government forces backed by Russian airpower retook Palmyra, the site of ancient ruins that ISIS had looted and partially destroyed.

The overstretched Syrian army lost Palmyra that December. But by that time Iraqi forces, backed by Peshmerga fighters and various militias drawn mostly from Iraq's minority communities and supported by coalition air power, had already begun their campaign to retake the crown jewel of ISIS's conquests: Mosul.

ISIS's ink-spot strategy also suffered setbacks. Unlike al-Qaeda, which can simply melt away when under attack, ISIS cannot act similarly because its strategy is to take and hold territory. While initially successful, ISIS affiliates soon faced American drone attacks and local resistance. This underscored the widely held opinion that ISIS's biggest problem in its attempt to expand outside Syria and Libya is that it does not play well with others: Rather than building alliances, ISIS insists on unconditional loyalty to the caliphate project and organizational uniformity. This is, more often than not, off-putting to potential partners.

ISIS affiliates lost ground in a number of places. In Libya, where ISIS was once likely to relocate if the caliphate in Syria and Iraq fell, ISIS lost Derna and Sirte and was thrown out of Benghazi by troops loyal to the internationally recognized Libyan government. Libya is important because of its proximity to Europe and Tunisia, which is a prime recruitment ground for the group. Libya is also important because it produces oil and straddles smuggling routes. In a similar fashion, the Taliban and the Algerian governments rolled up ISIS affiliates in Uzbekistan and Algeria, respectively; the Yemen ink spot collapsed as a result of internal feuding; and Boko Haram is well on its way to doing the same in West Africa.

At home, ISIS's caliphate has faced internal challenges as well that will likely prove insurmountable. The caliphate's financial model has proved to be unsustainable. According to insider estimates, as of April 2016, ISIS revenues were down 30 percent from the year before—from $80 million a month to $56 million. The reasons given for this fall-off range from the coalition bombing campaign, which targeted ISIS's oil production and smuggling operations, to the growing impoverishment of the population living under its rule, which limited its ability to extract revenue from them. As a result, ISIS had to slash salaries for its fighters by 50 percent. This has created a significant problem for ISIS because steady pay was one of the inducements it used to recruit local fighters. The recruitment of foreign fighters declined from 1,500 to 2,000 per month in spring 2015 to 200 per month a year later.

There are also indications that morale is down. So many fighters have fled its ranks that in October 2015, ISIS offered a general amnesty for deserters. Little wonder they left: ISIS executed fighters who had fled the battlefield in Kobani and Palmyra. ISIS's ranks are so depleted that it has taken to enlisting children, some as young as fourteen, into the "Cubs of the Caliphate." One deserter estimated that 60 percent of his unit was under the age of eighteen.

Even the caliphate's much vaunted singularity of purpose is under strain. In December 2015, ISIS leadership arrested members of a secret cell, whom it accused of plotting a coup. Their grievance? The Islamic State was not Islamic enough (one coup plotter pronounced *takfir* on al-Baghdadi because al-Baghdadi purportedly tolerated secular Muslims in order to milk them for revenue.) Others within the ranks have felt snubbed on the basis of nationality or ethnicity. Syrian fighters earn anywhere from one half to one quarter the salaries of foreign fighters. They are posted to dangerous front-line positions away from more comfortable urban centers where the foreigners are concentrated, and are disproportionately conscripted to fight on foreign battlefields, such as those in Libya. There have also been reports of fighting between Chechens and Arabs, again demonstrating that even within ISIS's ranks, ties of nationality, language, and ethnicity matter.

What happens to ISIS once its caliphate has disappeared?

Even if the caliphate's days are numbered, ISIS might continue to live on in one form or another. Experts have floated five possible scenarios for what the future might hold for the group.

The first scenario is that ISIS will go underground, only to reemerge at some point in the future. This scenario is not very likely because it ignores the unique set of circumstances that gave rise to ISIS and enabled it to win victory after victory in 2014: the political and military vacuum created by the Syrian civil war, the dysfunction of the Iraqi government of Nouri al-Maliki, the collapse of the Iraqi army, and the indifference of much of the world to the group's ambitions until it was too late. A similar set of circumstances is unlikely in the future.

Other experts have speculated that ISIS will simply set up shop elsewhere. This scenario, too, is unlikely because of the problems ISIS has encountered when it has tried to do so.

The third scenario predicts that ISIS fighters will continue to wage an insurgency in Syria or Iraq, or both. This is exactly what the Taliban did in Afghanistan after the American invasion in 2001. Indeed, after the American invasion of Iraq, al-Qaeda in Iraq and members of the disbanded Iraqi army did the same. This is a more likely scenario than the first two.

However, fighting an insurgency is quite a step down from establishing, defending, and expanding a territorial caliphate—what ISIS devotees consider an epochal event. And establishing, defending, and expanding a territorial caliphate is precisely what differentiates ISIS from al-Qaeda and similar groups. In the end, discordance between the goal of establishing a caliphate and fighting an insurgency may discourage those who signed on for the former from doing the latter.

It is, however, entirely feasible that ISIS fighters will continue the struggle. Revenge is a powerful motivator. But ISIS would no longer be ISIS were its fighters to limit their vision to waging a guerilla-style campaign. In fact, it would be no different from Jabhat al-Nusra, a group whose goals ISIS once abhorred.

There is also the possibility that ISIS fighters simply give up, or move on to other criminal enterprises. For true believers, the defeat of their caliphate might persuade them that their goal is unobtainable. It might therefore be extraordinarily dispiriting. Those who signed on for the thrill might find their kicks elsewhere, or merely fade back into the woodwork.

This too is a strong possibility, particularly if other nations besides Denmark offer their citizens who join ISIS the same incentives to return home the Danes offer to theirs. These incentives include pardons for those whose only crime was joining ISIS in the first place, career guidance, and psychological counseling. And this is in line with what other jihadi groups, such as al-Qaeda, have experienced as their members became disillusioned or discouraged or isolated.

Finally, it is entirely feasible that former fighters and freelancers will continue their attacks globally, with or without organizational backing. This too is a possibility, if only for a while. After all, a number of attacks outside of ISIS-held territory—including the attack in San Bernardino, California—occurred without the knowledge and assistance of ISIS. Of course, the destruction of ISIS's caliphate could reduce its capacity to produce and disseminate propaganda. This would diminish the group's ability to capture the imagination of would-be follow-ers in the future, although in the short term the world is not lacking in gullible and disturbed individuals.

Whatever the case, history provides lessons on how to deal effectively with movements and individuals who wage war against the international order. During the nineteenth and early-twentieth centuries, anarchists struck out at rulers and symbols of capitalism throughout the world. Anarchists assassinated the presidents of France and the United States, an empress of Austria, a king of Italy, and numerous government ministers in Russia. They also bombed symbols of oppression, from the haunts of the bourgeoisie to Wall Street itself.

Then, suddenly, the wave of anarchist violence ceased. By the onset of the Great Depression, anarchist activity was limited to a few isolated pockets, such as revolutionary Spain. Historians point to a number of reasons the anarchist moment passed: Anarchism competed for hearts and minds with other dissident groups; nations undertook political and social reforms that addressed the grievances of potential anar-chists and adopted new methods of policing and surveillance; and police agencies cooperated across borders. But perhaps the most important reason was that high-risk movements that attempt to realize the unrealizable have a short shelf life because potential recruits turn away from them. Such might be the case for ISIS.

5

PATRONS, PROXIES, AND FREELANCERS

THE INTERNATIONAL RELATIONS OF THE NEW MIDDLE EAST

How much did US strategy in the Middle East change under Barack Obama?

Measured on American terms, the United States was extraordinarily successful in the Middle East during the Cold War. Although it was not able to secure the peaceful resolution of all conflicts in the region—the Israel/Palestine dispute, for example, proved unsolvable—the United States successfully maintained a regional balance of power, ensured Western access to oil, protected the sea lanes and lines of communications, and safeguarded stable, pro-Western states in the region, including the State of Israel. Most important, by the end of the Cold War the United States had virtually locked the Soviet Union out of the Middle East. All the Soviets had to show for themselves were a few scattered allies in the region—Syria, Iraq, the People's Democratic Republic of Yemen—that were not particularly stable, reliable, or prosperous.

One of the most important reasons for—and measures of—American success in the Middle East is that the United States rarely directly intervened militarily in the region. It did not have to. Instead, the United States acted as what military analysts call an "offshore balancer." While according its regional partners a protective shield, the United States relied on them to check the ambitions of potentially hostile or disruptive states or non-state actors. In other words, the United States depended on its partners in the region to do the local policing. Pre-revolutionary Iran and Saudi Arabia acted as the "twin pillars," that protected the Gulf and the flow of oil. They contained Iraq. Israel provided for the defense of American interests to the west. It contained Syria.

Since most governments in the region supported the status quo, they worked hand in glove with the United States to thwart any changes in the state system, whether they were incited by communist-inspired insurgencies or by their unruly neighbors. In the early 1960s, North Yemeni republicans, supported by pro-Soviet Egypt, rebelled against the monarchists who held power. While Saudi Arabia and Jordan sent troops, President John F. Kennedy sent the Saudi king a personal message informing him that the United States would be there to uphold "Saudi Arabian integrity." When the Palestine Liberation Organization (PLO) threatened to overthrow the Jordanian government in 1970, Syrian tanks entered Jordan on the side of the PLO. The Syrian air force, however, did not provide them air cover, because the Israeli air force made its presence over Jordan known. To let the Israelis know the Americans had their back, the American Sixth Fleet steamed to the eastern Mediterranean. In the end, the Jordanian government prevailed.

There were, of course, a few American military forays into the region. Some were successful, some not. The United States intervened in Lebanon twice. The first time was in 1958, when it landed marines there to protect Lebanon from what the Lebanese president claimed was Egyptian subversion. They secured the port and airport, but they did not see any action. America's second intervention in Lebanon as part of a Multinational Force, however, ended disastrously. Originally deployed in 1983 as peacekeepers separating the PLO and Israel, the American troops, mostly Marines, suffered 241 fatalities when a suicide bomber blew up the barracks where they were sleeping. The US government ignominiously evacuated the remainder.

In the immediate aftermath of the Cold War, the United States led a military campaign supported by thirty-two countries to evict Iraq from Kuwait. That mission accomplished, the United States withdrew its forces. The Gulf War of 1991 lasted one hundred hours.

However quickly it was over, the Gulf War marked a subtle, episodic shift in American policy away from offshore balancing to direct intervention. During the Iran-Iraq War (1980–88), the United States had provided satellite intelligence (and maybe more) to the weaker Iraq so that it could continue a fight that preoccupied both countries. This prevented either one from dominating the Persian Gulf or making mischief elsewhere. But during the administration of Bill Clinton, the United States and its allies adopted a "dual containment" policy against Iran and Iraq. Instead of balancing the two states against each other, the United States tried to isolate them both at the same time.

The United States had imposed sanctions on Iran after its revolution and on Iraq after its invasion of Kuwait. During the Clinton years, these were bolstered and, in the case of Iraq, supplemented by occasional airstrikes. The purpose was either to get both regimes to change their ways or to encourage their overthrow. Dual containment depended on stationing forces nearby—Saudi Arabia—where the United States had stationed troops during the Gulf War. The policy failed: It was open ended, and both states found ways to reduce the impact of sanctions (which hurt the wrong people anyway and thus proved useful for anti-American propaganda). Since Saudi Arabia was home to the "holy sanctuaries" (the cities of Mecca and Medina), stationing troops there was provocative as well. Osama bin Laden, for example, gave the American presence on holy soil as one of the reasons for 9/11.

Worse was yet to come. Rather than going back to a policy of playing Iraq and Iran against each other, the United States gave Iran a gift by invading Iraq in 2003 and overthrowing Saddam Hussein. Iraq crumbled into chaos. Not only was it no longer a formidable foe that would act as a military bulwark against Iran, it became a breeding ground for jihadi groups that would threaten the United States and its allies. It also became a venue for Iranian meddling.

Just why the United States abandoned the winning strategy of offshore balancing is not clear. It is likely that a number of US policy makers saw the collapse of the Soviet Union as an opportunity for the world's sole remaining superpower to flex its muscles and shape the world according to its own interests and values. Some, known as neoconservatives, believed the United States could ignore the niceties of international law and international institutions and impose its will unilaterally, by force if necessary. Neoconservatives were responsible for America's Iraq adventure. Others, known as liberal internationalists, also believed "American values" should be applied universally, but believed that this should be done by working within the framework of international law and international institutions. Liberal internationalists were responsible for the United States' participation in the bombing campaign to oust Muammar Qaddafi in Libya. They also advocated a more direct American role in the Syrian civil war.

After he took office, Barack Obama wanted to restore offshore balancing. This is why, for example, he pledged support for efforts made by the GCC to build their collective self-defense capabilities, including the installation of a collective antiballistic missile shield. Although the shield is intended to protect the GCC member states from incoming Iranian missiles, they have only half-heartedly signed on to it. Instead, they prefer the United States make a NATO-like commitment to defend them if attacked.

Economists refer to something they call the "free rider problem." Free riders are those who contribute nothing, but take advantage of a common good for which others pay. For the states of the Gulf, choosing between free riding and offshore balancing by the United States is an easy call.

What has happened between the United States and its partners in the region?

After President Obama actually called out America's European and Arab partners as "free riders," Prince Turki al-Faisal, the former ambassador of Saudi Arabia to the United States and member of Saudi Arabia's ruling family, wrote an open rejoinder on the pages of *Arab News*. It began, "No, Mr. Obama. We are not 'free riders.'"[1] He then went on to list the ways Saudi policies benefit the United States. Four of those policies in particular stand out for their audacity: "we train and fund the Syrian freedom fighters"; "[we] initiated the support . . . that is helping the Yemeni people reclaim their country from the murderous militia, the Houthis"; "[we] established a coalition of more than thirty Muslim countries to fight all shades of terrorism in the world"; and, most bizarrely, "[we] combat extremist ideology that attempts to hijack our religion, on all levels." Here's what he left out:

- True, the Saudis train and fund Syrian "freedom fighters." Unfortunately, many of the groups the Saudis support are little better than Jabhat Fateh al-Sham, the latest incarnation of the al-Qaeda affiliate Jabhat al-Nusra, and many are salafi.
- The Saudis certainly did initiate a war against the Houthis in Yemen, but the United States was an unwilling partner in that war, which it viewed as unnecessary and unwinnable. It went along with Saudi Arabia in an effort to try to prevent them from sabotaging the nuclear deal with Iran, which they tried to do anyway.
- It is, of course, in the American interest for the Saudis to put together a coalition to fight terrorism. But this coalition is mainly aimed at uniting Sunni countries against Shi'i Iran at a time the United States, bowing to what it believed to be the inevitable, was trying to bring Iran into international councils. In the American view, it is better

to make Iran a stakeholder in the international system than an outlier from it intent on doing mischief.

- The coalition is also aimed at subverting Muslim Brotherhood–style movements, which the Saudis view as a threat. The Saudi policy that Muslims should passively obey their leaders—part of the Saudi dynasty's survival strategy—naturally put Saudi Arabia at odds with all politically minded Islamists. This is the reason Saudi Arabia funded the military coup d'état against the legally elected Muslim Brotherhood government of Egypt—a government recognized by the United States.

- Finally, the claim that Saudi Arabia combats extremist ideology clearly merits the use of the word "bizarre." According to estimates, from the 1960s through 2017, Saudi Arabia has spent approximately $100 billion spreading the venomous doctrine of Wahhabism through schools, mosques, the media, and money. For sake of comparison, from 1920 through 1991 the Soviet Union spent an estimated $7 billion spreading communist ideology. Wahhabism has squeezed out other, more moderate forms of Islam. In many places in the Middle East it is the only game in town. Wahhabism conflicts with values many Americans hold dear (women's rights, popular sovereignty) and acts as the gateway drug for many who go on to become jihadis.

As absurd as many of the points the prince makes are, his op-ed demonstrates the problem that has dogged America's relationship with its partners in the region since the end of the Cold War. During the Cold War, America's overriding interest was to keep the Soviet Union out of the region and maintain the status quo there. That, too, was in the interest of America's partners. After all, any change in the status quo might threaten their regimes or even their states. But after the collapse of the Soviet Union that overriding interest was gone, and the United States and its partners diverged in terms of what they considered to be their national interests and how to go about achieving them.

For example, America's Arab partners grew accustomed to American support no matter what they did domestically. So even though the support the United States gave to the Arab uprisings was tepid (with the exception of Libya), the fact that the United States did not go to the mat for autocrats it had once supported shocked and angered them. That can be seen in the well-worn but false Saudi refrain that the United States had thrown Hosni Mubarak under a bus (in fact, while the Obama administration policy was evolving from continued support of Mubarak to calling for a transition government that would include him, the Egyptian people were busy throwing him under a bus). And when Bashar al-Assad used chemical weapons on his own people—thus crossing Obama's "red line"—and the United States inflicted no punishment on him for doing so, the Saudis (and others) were apoplectic that the United States had refrained from involving itself directly in the Syrian imbroglio.

It is not just in the Arab world where American interests and the interests of its partners in the region—both real and perceived—diverged. Take Israel. The Obama administration, like almost every administration since the time of Dwight D. Eisenhower, subscribed to the doctrine of "linkage." For them, every problem in the Middle East can be linked to the Israel-Palestine conflict, either directly or indirectly (in terms of the latter, policy makers making the connection sometimes have to use a rationale reminiscent of "Six Degrees of Kevin Bacon"). Therefore, resolving the conflict became an imperative for administration after administration—that is, until each administration got burned and moved on.

Over the years, however, Israel became more right wing, nationalistic, and religiously orthodox than it had been before the 1967 war. In particular, as a result of the war the Israelis came to occupy the Palestinian territories, and what to do with those territories came to occupy the center stage of Israeli politics. During the 1980s, Israeli politicians on the right formed an alliance with the so-called settler movement, which is composed of those Israelis who want to retain and "settle"—colonize—the territories. They balked at making any agreement brokered by the United States that might force Israel to disgorge them. Thus, short-term political calculus trumped what American policy makers, rightly or wrongly, believed to be in America's (and Israel's) national interest.

Israel, like Saudi Arabia, views Iran—particularly a nuclear-armed Iran—as an existential threat. It had reason. Not only has Iran supported Hizbullah, a former Iranian president once quoted Iran's first post-revolution leader as stating that Israel "must be wiped out from the map of the world."[2] Israel, like Saudi Arabia, did what it could to scuttle the nuclear deal that the so-called P5 + 1 countries (members of the UN Security Council plus the European Union) brokered with Iran. For them, it was not strong enough because it did not dismantle Iran's nuclear program in its entirety; rather, it delayed and diminished it. Both countries urged the United States not to sign the deal; instead, they urged the United States to take other steps—including military action, if necessary—to prevent Iran from enriching weapons-grade uranium. The Israeli prime minister, Benjamin Netanyahu, even bypassed the president of the United States and took his case directly to the US Congress.

The United States signed the deal anyway. The Obama administration perceived nuclear proliferation not only to be a threat to the peace of the region, but an existential threat to the United States. It certainly did not want a nuclear arms race in the Middle East.

Finally, there's Turkey, a NATO ally and a state that has become increasingly autocratic (and accelerated the march to autocracy after an attempted coup d'état in July 2016 gave Turkish president Recep Tayyip Erdogan [pronounced *Er*-do-wan] the pretext to do so). Like Saudi Arabia, Turkey has backed some pretty unsavory groups in Syria. As a matter of fact, Turkey and the United States have nurtured relationships with two very different varieties of groups in the Syrian civil war: Turkey has worked closely with the Islamist opposition, the United States, with Kurdish groups. Turkey views those groups, whose quest for an autonomous or independent Syrian Kurdistan might inspire Turkey's own Kurds to seek the same, as an existential threat. The United States, on the other hand, has depended on the Kurds in its war against ISIS (a group which Donald Trump and some of his advisers believe poses an existential threat to the United States).

As in the case of Saudi Arabia and Israel, there is little likelihood Turkey will sever its long-standing relationship with the world's foremost military and economic power. There are too many shared interests—from the economic and political to the institutional—binding them together. There have been rough patches in America's relationship with all three before: the king of Saudi Arabia, incensed by comments made by George W. Bush about tilting toward Israel in the Israeli-Palestinian conflict, refused an invitation to visit him; the United States has opposed Israeli military actions and settlement activities on a number of occasions; and the United States clamped an arms embargo on Turkey after it invaded Cyprus in 1974. (Contrary to popular belief, Barack Obama's administration was not the first to have abstained or supported UN resolutions critical of Israel; for example, George W. Bush's allowed six such resolutions to pass, George H. W. Bush's allowed nine, and Ronald Reagan's allowed twenty-one.)

Nevertheless, since Saudi Arabia, Israel, and Turkey perceive their interests as conflicting with American interests in a variety of realms, those relationships may prove to be rockier in the future than in the past.

Did Obama have a strategy for the Middle East?

According to inside accounts, when Barack Obama became president in 2009, the prevailing view among his foreign policy staff was that the United States had expended far too much time and effort on Middle East issues during the administration of George W. Bush and far too little time and effort on Asia. Asia, they believed, would be the epicenter of global competition in the twenty-first century. Obama therefore intended to extricate the United States from the Middle East so it might "pivot to Asia," the region that would not only be the fulcrum of global affairs in the future, but one in which American endeavors might more readily bear fruit.

The Arab uprisings, the Syrian civil war, and the rise of ISIS made that pivot impossible. Nevertheless, Obama remained committed to at least lightening the American footprint in the Middle East. That is why the United States participated in the NATO air campaign in Libya but did not stick around afterward to pick up the pieces, why Obama backed away from the red line he had drawn in Syria, and why the United States offered only limited support to the Saudi war against the Houthis in Yemen. That is also why Obama pledged to end the wars in Afghanistan and Iraq. The sole exception to the lighter-footprint policy was launching a war against ISIS.

The United States had invaded Afghanistan after 9/11 because its government harbored Osama bin Laden. Although it would have been more logical simply to go after bin Laden and call it a day, the administration of George W. Bush decided to replace the government of Afghanistan as well—a far more costly and difficult task. As far as Iraq was concerned, the Bush administration had come up with various rationales to justify the invasion: the Iraqi government collaborated with al-Qaeda, Iraq possessed weapons of mass destruction, a free and democratic Iraq would provide an example that other states in the region would emulate. Whatever the rationale du jour, a number of critics—from former Secretary of State James Baker to the British commission tasked to do a postmortem on the war—have identified it as "an unnecessary war of choice."[3] Obama had been elected in part because of his opposition to the war.

The policy makers who had led the United States into Iraq saw the war as a means to demonstrate American strength and hegemony in a post–Cold War world. Obama took the opposite view. He believed the war sapped American strength and prestige. And because the United States flouted international conventions and norms in launching and waging it, he believed the war diminished America's moral standing in the world.

By the time Obama took office, close to 5,000 American soldiers had died in the two wars. Between 2001 and 2009, Congress had appropriated almost a trillion dollars to wage them. The American campaigns were open ended and Obama wanted out. The United States completed its withdrawal from Iraq in December 2011. It began withdrawing its forces from Afghanistan around the same time.

The wars in Iraq and Afghanistan were not the only wars being fought when Obama took office. A little over a week after 9/11, George W. Bush declared the Global War on Terrorism. "Our war on terror begins with al Qaeda, but it does not end there. It will not end until every terrorist group of global reach has been found, stopped and defeated."[4] While GWOT was overwhelmingly popular in a country that had just experienced the trauma of 9/11, a number of commentators viewed it with skepticism. Terrorism is not an enemy per se, they argued; rather, it is a tactic used by America's enemies. Furthermore, like other wars on common nouns—the War on Poverty, the War on Drugs—there will be no point at which the United States would be able to say "mission accomplished" and proclaim victory. Policing, they maintained, not declarations of war, was the only way to deal with terrorism.

Obama seems to have agreed with the skeptics. But he also saw the price paid by the Democratic presidential candidate, John Kerry, in 2004 when he called al-Qaeda "a nuisance" and equated its actions with crimes like prostitution and gambling—crimes which will never be eliminated, however much they might be minimized. Kerry lost. Obama also knew the political price he'd have to pay should there have been another large-scale attack on the United States.

Obama chose anyway to de-escalate GWOT, which he re-branded "overseas contingency operations"[5]—a phrase without the word "war." He also attempted to reduce the American footprint by expanding the use of drones and Special Forces. (To Obama's critics, using drones to kill leaders of terrorist groups is counterproductive. They claim that "collateral damage"—civilian casualties—fans anti-American flames, that assassinations undermine America's moral position in the world, and that killing "leaders" of what are, in fact, semiautonomous, self-organizing networks that can always reconstitute their leadership is of doubtful value.) While these tactics did degrade al-Qaeda, the emergence of ISIS, its threat to the regional order, and the globalization of its terror operations compelled Obama to escalate antiterror operations in the region and initiate a campaign to destroy the chief purveyor of terrorism both there and beyond. It also compelled him to reintroduce American forces into Iraq after they had been withdrawn.

Obama's reversal of course betrays an inherent problem the United States faced in realizing his strategic vision in the Middle East. Not only did some policies just plain fail, but American policy makers were also blindsided by events, some of which they could not have foreseen, others of which wishful thinking or obtuseness prevented them from seeing. The former category includes not only the Arab uprisings, the Syrian civil war, and the rise of ISIS, but also the Turkish drift to authoritarianism and Russian assertion. The latter includes the Israeli pushback against a freeze in settlement expansion on Palestinian land and the Saudi pushback against any number of American policies. Unfortunately, policy makers did not prove themselves particularly nimble when confronted by errant events, nor were there any guideposts for them to follow in this brave new world.

But there is a more fundamental reason American policy makers have not been able to secure the Middle East of their dreams so that they might turn their attention elsewhere: The underlying problems facing the region are not the sorts of problems the United States (or any other power) is adept at solving. This prevents the United States from offering up some quick fix and moving on. During the Cold War, the United States could be impervious to those underlying problems and rely on its military might to resolve or deter its way through the challenges it confronted. The challenges the New Middle East presents—the proliferation of non-state actors, failed governments, stagnant economies, the ravages of environmental degradation and global warming—cannot be resolved through the application of military force. Unfortunately, military force is the one tool the United States wields with assurance.

What was America's policy toward Iran under Obama?

Under Obama, American policies in the Middle East met as often with failure as with success. Nevertheless, he did achieve what he and administration supporters viewed as a significant step toward preventing a nuclear arms race in the region. In his first inaugural address, Obama promised America's adversaries that he would "extend a hand if you are willing to unclench your fist."[6] Obama had one Middle Eastern fist in particular in mind: Iran's. Obama believed that relaxing tensions with Iran and bringing it into the regional order would calm the waters and make it possible to resolve some of America's more intractable problems. There was only one way to achieve this while soothing the fears of America's traditional partners in the Middle East: The international community had to convince Iran to end or defer its quest for nuclear weapons.

Negotiations between Iran and the P5 + 1 countries over the future of Iran's nuclear program began in 2006, even before Obama assumed office. Negotiators finally struck a deal in July 2015. While the deal does not prevent Iran from enriching uranium (in other words, upgrading uranium to make it usable in a bomb), it does limit Iran to enriching uranium below "weapons grade" for fifteen years. It also includes provisions to prevent Iran from cheating and to ensure continued international inspection of its nuclear facilities. In return, the P5 + 1 countries removed economic sanctions that had crippled the Iranian economy. In spite of both foreign and domestic opposition, the Obama administration signed on to the deal two months later.

Obama publicly downplayed the "game changing" role of the Iran nuclear deal. He decoupled the deal from any further understandings or cooperation with Iran and assured America's partners in the region it was a one-off. Nevertheless, the nuclear deal effectively broke the diplomatic ice between Iran and the United States. When the United Nations invited Iran to the Geneva III negotiations on the Syrian civil war, the United States didn't squawk, nor did it block Iranian participation as it had earlier. Iran even participated in the vetting of the opposition negotiating team to prevent the presence of "terrorists" on it—although few in Washington, DC, were amused by its suggestion that the CIA be added to the list of terrorist organizations to be excluded. As a result, the deal did set a precedent, which both sides acknowledged obliquely. As Barack Obama put it in the wake of the nuclear deal with Iran, Saudi Arabia had "to find an effective way to share the neighborhood and institute some sort of cold peace."[7]

What role does oil play in the New Middle East?

From June 2014 to April 2016, oil prices dropped 70 percent. Economists gave a number of reasons for the drop. Some reasons they cited were temporary aberrations. One such aberration was a downturn in the Chinese economy, which decreased demand in the world's second-largest consumer of imported oil. Another was deliberate Saudi overproduction to drive oil prices down in order to hurt the economies of Saudi Arabia's Russian and Iranian competitors. But some reasons for the drop in prices will not go away soon. For example, more oil was available not only because of Saudi Arabia, but because Iraq, the second-largest oil producer in the Organization of Petroleum Exporting Countries, rebounded from its torpor and produced record amounts. Iranian oil also contributed to the glut. After Iran signed the nuclear agreement, the international community removed the sanctions that had taken Iranian oil off the market.

Perhaps the most troubling news for oil exporters, however, came from the United States. New technologies, such as horizontal drilling and fracking (breaking up subterranean rock to release oil and natural gas) made the United States the world's largest oil producer. And while the United States increased production, domestic demand in the world's largest oil consumer also fell. American oil consumption was lower in 2015 than it had been in 1997, mainly as a result of increased fuel efficiency in cars. That holy grail of American politics, energy independence, seemed at last to be within reach.

As of 2015, the United States still imported 60 percent of the oil it consumed, but only a fraction of it came from the Gulf. In fact, the United States imported four times as much oil from the Western hemisphere as it did from the Gulf. In theory, less dependence on Gulf oil means greater maneuverability for the United States when formulating policy toward Iran and the rest of the Middle East. It just won't matter as much if down the road some Middle Eastern king gets his nose out of joint.

It is difficult to predict whether the collapse in oil prices is a passing blip or a long-term trend. Most economists think the price of oil will rebound, although not to peak levels. But this hasn't prevented oil-producing states from following the advice of the IMF to take steps to diversify their economies. The IMF has recommended that Gulf producers bolster science, technology, and vocational education; target specific sectors and industries for investment (the financial sector in Bahrain, petrochemicals and mining in Saudi Arabia); put money into infrastructure; strengthen their legal and regulatory environment; and encourage entrepreneurship and innovation by expanding access to information. The theory is that this will stimulate the private sector and move GCC countries toward an export model like Japan.

The Saudi government, for one, has taken the IMF's recommendations to heart. In spring 2016, Deputy Crown Prince Muhammad bin Salman unveiled a plan titled "Vision 2030," prepared by an American consulting firm, McKinsey & Co. "Vision 2030" is more of a retread than a vision. It includes a list of off-the-shelf neo-liberal recommendations that might just as well have been prepared for the government of Peru. The plan calls for privatizing government assets, including education and 5 percent of the national oil company, Saudi Aramco; reducing and targeting subsidies on oil, electricity, and water; introducing an income tax; and creating 450,000 new private sector jobs.

The odds that Saudi Arabia is capable of transforming its economy within less than two decades to become globally competitive are, at best, a long shot. It means unilaterally redefining the ruling bargain that connects the Saudi population with its government. It means discarding the most effective tool the government has to gain the consent of their population—buying it. It means ensuring a free flow of information in a country that, in 2016, Reporters Without Borders ranked 165th out of 180 countries surveyed in terms of press freedom—a country in which transparency on all levels of governance and commerce is rare.[8] (Does Saudi Arabia, a country in which the royal family uses its most valuable asset as a dynastic piggy bank, really intend to open up the books of Saudi Aramco to attract potential investors? Finally, it means changing attitudes toward work in a country in which women make up only 22 percent of the workforce and foreigners literally do all the heavy lifting.

What are the roots of the Saudi-Iranian competition?

Since the outbreak of the Arab uprisings in 2010, Saudi Arabia and Iran have been on opposite sides in a number of civil conflicts and political disputes besides the one in Syria.

- The Iranians support Hizbullah in Lebanon. In addition to the shared goal of keeping Israel off balance, leaders from Iran and Hizbullah have built personal relationships dating back to the days when they studied theology together at the shrine cities of Najaf and Karbala in Iraq. The Iranians have used Syria as a land bridge to arm Hizbullah and have provided it with sophisticated missiles that the group has used against Israel. The Saudis, on the other hand, have supported the Sunni-dominated Future Movement in Lebanon, which compelled Syria to remove the remainder of its forces that had occupied that country since 1976, the second year of the Lebanese civil war. The Saudis have also provided financial assistance to build the Lebanese army as a counterweight to Hizbullah and were behind the declaration by the Arab League pronouncing Hizbullah a terrorist organization.
- In Iraq, the Iranians have thrown their weight behind a number of Shi'i politicians, including former Prime Minister Nouri al-Maliki (who, ironically, had been a favorite of the Americans because of his supposed independence from Iran) and his successor, Haidar al-Abadi, along with various Shi'i parties and militias involved in the fight against ISIS. On the other hand, the relationship between post-occupation Iraq and Saudi Arabia has ranged from cool to frigid. The Saudis considered al-Maliki to be an Iranian agent and disapproved strongly of his Shi'i-dominated government. During the American occupation, they had provided assistance to Sunni fighters, some of whom ended up fighting the Americans.
- The Saudis saw an Iranian footprint in the Bahraini uprising of 2011, where it did not exist, and launched a war in Yemen to fight the Houthi insurgency, claiming that Iran was behind it. Most commentators note that the Houthi insurgency, which began in 2004, was stirred by local grievances and that initially the Iranian role was minimal.

- The Saudis have also confronted Iran diplomatically. The Saudis opposed the P5 + 1 deal with the Iranians, fearing that it would bring Iran out of isolation. Saudi Arabia also opposed tiny Qatar's balancing act between its two larger neighbors and led an international movement to boycott it. And after Iranians stormed the Saudi embassy in Tehran (incited by the Saudi execution of a prominent Saudi Shi'i cleric), the Saudis not only broke off diplomatic relations with Iran, they "encouraged" Bahrain, Kuwait, the UAE, and Sudan to downgrade or cut ties also.

A number of commentators trace the Saudi-Iranian competition in the region to the Sunni-Shi'i split that divided the Islamic community after the death of Muhammad in A.D. 632 (actually, Shi'ism as a separate sect dates from about 130 years later). History, however, tells us something different. There have been long periods of time when Shi'is and Sunnis lived together without problems. In fact, at the time of the American invasion of Iraq, marriages between Sunnis and Shi'is represented approximately 30 percent of all marriages there. Sectarianism is not the universal default position for Muslims. It is no more natural for Muslims to fuse their religious identity with their political identity than it is for anyone else. Sectarianism can always be traced to political entrepreneurs who transform communal solidarity into a demand for rights, set-asides, or even autonomy. Those entrepreneurs might be individuals, groups and parties, or even governments.

There have been times when governments of Sunni-dominated lands shared interests and cooperated with governments of Shi'i-dominated lands. Before the Iranian Revolution, the United States viewed Iran and Saudi Arabia as its "twin pillars" in the Gulf. After the revolution, Iran allied itself with Hamas, the (Sunni) Palestinian group that dominates Gaza in its confrontation with Israel (since Hamas allied itself with the opposition in Syria, relations have not been as close as they used to be). And the bloodiest war of the post–World War II period pitted Iran against Iraq—two predominantly Shi'i states. In spite of predictions to the contrary, Shi'is living in Iraq and Sunnis (and Arabs) living in Iran remained loyal to their respective governments.

Finally, if the hostility between Saudi Arabia and Iran were a dispute between Sunnis and Shi'is, one would expect Sunni Turkey to ally itself with Sunni Saudi Arabia against Shi'i Iran. Of course, Turkey and Iran *have been* on opposite sides in the Syrian civil war, and Turkey *does* maintain good relations with the states of the GCC. Nevertheless, Turkey and Iran are currently enjoying cordial relations, while Saudi-Iranian relations are at their lowest point since 1979. Turkey and Iran enjoy a strong economic relationship, and both oppose Kurdish aspirations, which, they believe, threaten the integrity of their countries. On the other hand, as often as not, Turkey and Saudi Arabia act at cross-purposes in the region. The Turks, for example, supported various Muslim Brotherhood movements during the 2010–11 uprisings. The Saudis opposed them.

If the current Saudi-Iranian animosity is not about religion per se, what, then, is it about? Simply put, it's about politics. Saudi Arabia and Iran (along with Turkey) operate on different models of governance, have different goals in the region, and have different survival strategies.

Saudi Arabia promotes submission to the dynasty at home and adherence to the status quo abroad. The Saudi government does not like to see Islamic activism anywhere because it threatens that status quo. Saudi Arabia has also been aligned with the United States, the dominant status quo power in the world and the guarantor of the Middle East state system. Finally, Saudi Shi'is are concentrated in the Eastern Province of Saudi Arabia, where the oil is. That population is impoverished, faces discrimination and repression, and has been restive. The Saudi government fears that Saudi Arabia's Shi'is might act as an Iranian fifth column against it.

The profile of Iran is the polar opposite of that of Saudi Arabia. A staunch ally of the United States in the region before the revolution of 1978–79, Iranian foreign policy flipped 180 degrees after it.

The newly established Islamic Republic viewed itself as a revolutionary power intent on shaking up the status quo and defying and rolling back American imperialism. While in its rhetoric and actions it has largely backed away from spreading the revolutionary model, it has taken advantage of cracks in the system, particularly those that might be traced to the Arab uprisings. Iran's reach has been exaggerated by Saudi Arabia—what better way for the Saudis to rally domestic and foreign support than to raise a cry of alarm? Nevertheless, Iran has responded positively to the 2010–11 uprisings and protests (with the notable exception of Syria) that have challenged the old order in the Arab world. That old order has involved the oppression of Shi'is in a number of places in the region. Iran thus has had both causes to champion and groups to which it could appeal on the basis of communal solidarity.

Nevertheless, while both Saudi Arabia and Iran have, since 2010, played the sectarian card to gain allies and thus advantage in their struggle for dominance, the Saudis have played it more aggressively than the Iranians. This only stands to reason: During the Obama administration, the Saudis felt more vulnerable than ever before—whether that feeling was justified or not.

Before Obama, Saudi Arabia counted on the United States to be there if an existential threat arose. When Obama was in office, the Saudis suspected the American commitment to their defense and feared abandonment. With Obama as president, the Saudi stance in the face of danger was no longer, as it had been since the 1990s, to crawl under the table and wait for the arrival of the American cavalry. They became proactive, financially, diplomatically, and militarily. (Interestingly, the Trump administration has subscribed to the Saudi line that the greatest threat in the region is terrorism and that Iran is terrorism's greatest purveyor. It can therefore be assumed that so long as Saudi Arabia continues to set the American agenda it is likely to remain proactive.)

In addition, the Arab uprisings have fed Saudi feelings of vulnerability because they threaten or have threatened to upset the status quo. Saudi Arabia has seen the governments of close allies, such as Bahrain and Yemen, endangered or removed, and its own under threat. And it has not just been the uprisings that have threatened the balance in the region. Although there was no love lost between Saudi Arabia and Saddam Hussein, his replacement by a Shi'i-dominated government that is close to Iran has been a bitter pill to swallow.

What is Turkey's role in the New Middle East?

The parliamentary election of 2002 was a watershed moment in Turkish politics. The Justice and Development Party, at the time heralded as a moderate Islamist party, won two-thirds of the seats, and its leader, Recep Erdogan, became prime minister. Not only did this victory signal another step in the death march of Kemalism—the secular nationalism that was the official ideology since the birth of the republic—it marked a transformation of Turkish foreign policy.

During the previous decades, Turkey had oriented toward the West, and Turkey's grand ambition was to join the European Union as a full member. While Turkey's new government did not abandon this ambition, it also sought to strengthen ties with its neighbors in the Middle East and Caucasus. This policy was called the "zero problems with neighbors" policy. The Turkish government reached out to its Arab neighbors, Russia, Iran, and even its old nemesis, Armenia (to no avail). Some even talked of a New Ottomanism, an orientation that recalled the Istanbul-based empire that governed Anatolia, the Asiatic Arab world, and Egypt until its demise in 1922. At first, the "zero problems with neighbors" policy appeared to be a success. Estranged or neglected relationships warmed, and Turkey even tried its hand at mediation, brokering talks between Israel and Syria, the two wings of the Palestinian national movement, and Afghanistan and Pakistan.

Then came the Arab uprisings of 2010–11. Unlike Saudi Arabia, which viewed the uprisings as a calamity in the making, the Turkish government viewed them as an opportunity to promote like-minded moderate Islamic populist regimes throughout the region. American policy makers agreed, with some enthusiastically endorsing the "Turkish model" for melding Western-style democracy with Islam. This, they believed, would guarantee popular support for democratic institutions in the Arab world. Saudi Arabia was, of course, appalled.

Having thus alienated Saudi Arabia and its GCC allies, the Turks went about alienating virtually everyone else. Turkey was an early supporter of the Muslim Brotherhood government in Egypt and, for a while, friendship with Egypt became the cornerstone of Turkish foreign policy. When the military overthrew that government, the Turks condemned the coup d'état. The new Egyptian government broke off relations. The internationally recognized government of Libya, furious because of Ankara's support for Islamist groups there, did likewise. Turkey's support for the opposition in Syria naturally alienated that government. Its lackluster efforts to prevent ISIS fighters en route to Iraq from crossing its border with Syria alienated the Iraqis as well. So did Turkey's purchases of oil from the Kurdish Regional Government in Iraq—purchases that the Iraqi central government never sanctioned.

Turkey also got into spats with Israel and Russia. The Turkish government was furious when Israeli commandos assaulted a ship filled with Turkish passengers, killing ten Turkish citizens. The ship, sailing in international waters, was carrying humanitarian assistance and construction materials to Palestinians in Gaza. The incident underscored deteriorating relations between the two countries, which the Israelis blamed on Islamist inspired anti-Semitism and the Turks blamed on Israel's harsh policies against the Palestinians. Russia and Turkey found themselves on opposite sides in the Syrian civil war, and it didn't help that Turkey shot down a Russian warplane that overflew Turkish territory. In sum, Turkey's "zero problems with neighbors" policy became Turkey's "zero friends" policy.

Turkey began a charm offensive in 2015 to win back some of those friends. It struck agreements with both Israel and Russia, and Algeria brokered talks between Turkey and Syria. But by summer 2016 Turkey had little time to focus on its external relations. The war against the PKK that reignited in 2015 devastated Turkey's southeast and so inflamed Kurdish sentiment there that the Turkish government decided to move two provincial capitals in that area to other, safer locations. Then there was the attempted coup d'état against Erdogan in July 2016. Although it failed miserably, the coup provided an excuse for the Erdogan government to impose a state of emergency and purge the military, the bureaucracy, the media, and even academia. Within a month, tens of thousands lost their jobs and one hundred media outlets were shut down. Overall, then, Turkey's inward focus and self-inflicted wounds make it an unlikely contender for regional leader in the near future.

Whatever happened to the Israel-Palestine conflict?

From December 1992 through August 1993, an unofficial delegation of Israelis met with a delegation of Palestinians in Oslo, Norway. In talks hosted by the Norwegian foreign minister and his wife, they hammered out a formula for peace between Israelis and Palestinians, known ever since as the Oslo Accord. Once the negotiators had put together a general framework, they presented it for official consideration.

The Oslo Accord signed by the Israeli government and the PLO includes two separate protocols. The first consists of an exchange of letters of mutual recognition between the two parties: The PLO recognized the State of Israel; Israel recognized the PLO as the representative of the Palestinian people. The second protocol stipulated that Israel and the PLO would negotiate a limited withdrawal of Israeli troops from the West Bank and Gaza—the first of what was to be further withdrawals. It also stipulated that the Palestinians would take steps to establish a governing body (the Palestinian Authority) which would enter into "permanent status negotiations" with Israel. The seemingly intractable conflict would thus be over, with two states living side by side in peace and security, as diplomats liked to say.

Of course, the devil was in the details. Decades later, there is still no settlement. During those decades there have been brief episodes of frenetic negotiation, interrupted by brief episodes of intense violence, interrupted by longer periods of inactivity. In the meantime, Israel has continued to expand its settlements in the West Bank.

At one time or another, each side walked away from the Oslo process and attempted to impose a solution unilaterally. At the beginning of the twenty-first century, Israel withdrew from Gaza, which for the Israelis had little value. It also constructed a separation barrier—a "security fence"—between the territory it claimed for itself and the West Bank territory that would remain outside its borders. The barrier snakes deep into Palestinian territory on the West Bank, and includes within Israeli territory Jerusalem and most of the settlement blocs. For Israelis, the path of the barrier was meant to demarcate Israel's permanent boundaries and constitute the final act in the conflict. But it was not to be: In 2006 rockets launched from Gaza and Lebanon and aimed at Israel convinced most Israelis that the separation barrier could not guarantee their safety. The Israeli experiment in unilateralism ended.

The Palestinians, too, had their bout of unilateralism. In the wake of an uprising that threatened not just his government but the entire edifice of Palestinian self-rule, Palestinian president Mahmoud Abbas pushed for United Nations recognition of a

Palestinian state. What he got instead was recognition of Palestine as a "non-voting member entity." And nothing changed.

What perhaps is most surprising about the current state of the conflict is how it has moved from the center stage of political concern in the region to a sideshow. Coalitions of Arab states went to war against Israel three times—1948, 1967, and 1973 (there were other wars as well). Both the 1948 and 1967 wars were regional conflagrations. The 1973 war had global economic and diplomatic ramifications. It also led to the most dangerous confrontation between the United States and the Soviet Union since the Cuban Missile Crisis. But recent developments—the Arab uprisings, the Syrian civil war, the rise of ISIS—have made the longest-running unresolved conflict on the planet yesterday's news. Whether Israelis and Palestinians, who together make up less than 3 percent of the population of the Middle East, make peace or not has paled in significance when compared with other problems facing the region.

And those other problems have had a curious effect on the status of Israel in the region. The Israeli-Palestinian conflict, which stretches back to 1881, has always been a conflict between two peoples—Israelis and their ancestors, on the one hand, and Palestinians and theirs, on the other. Even during the 1948–93 period, when most of the world chose to view the conflict as one between states and believed that once those states had made peace it would be over, it was, at its heart, a conflict between two peoples. This fact has never been clearer than in the wake of the 2010–11 uprisings, when Israel and the GCC countries—particularly Saudi Arabia—found themselves strategically aligned on multiple issues, including Iran and Syria. Since then, there have been unofficial meetings between high-ranking Israelis and their Saudi counterparts on several occasions. Whether the current alignment continues, or the Israeli government decides to forsake it by, for example, annexing to Israel parts of the West Bank unilaterally, remains to be seen.

6

HUMAN SECURITY IN THE NEW MIDDLE EAST

What is "human security"?

When the term "security" is used among policy makers and political scientists, more often than not it refers to the security of states, not the security of those who live within them. The term "human security" was therefore invented to shift the focus to those factors that make populations unsafe as the first step to rendering them less so. According to the United Nations Development Programme (UNDP), human security is "the liberation of human beings from those intense, extensive, prolonged, and comprehensive threats to which their lives and freedom are vulnerable."[1]

In 2009, the UNDP published *The Arab Human Development Report: Challenges to Human Security in the Arab Countries*. The report lists seven "dimensions" of the threat to human security in the Arab world: "people and their insecure environment"; "the state and its insecure people"; "the vulnerability of those lost from sight"; "volatile growth, high unemployment and persisting poverty"; "hunger, malnutrition and food insecurity"; "health security challenges"; and "occupation and military intervention." Needless to say, the Arab world and, indeed, the Middle East as a whole are regions in which the threats to human security are among the greatest in the world.

There are two problems, however, with measuring human security in the Middle East as a whole. First, the Arab region currently tends to be more vulnerable to certain types of threats to human security than its non-Arab neighbors. Among them are political instability and the breakdown of states, proxy wars and foreign interventions, the spread of sectarianism, huge increases in refugee flows, economic stagnation, an overdependence on income from rent, an insecure food supply, and the inability of states to adapt successfully to the neo-liberal blueprint or to take advantage of globalization (with the exception of sub-Saharan Africa, the Arab region is the least globalized region in the world). The second problem with measuring human security in the region as a whole is that the non-Arab majority states in the region, particularly Israel, are exceptional in a number of ways.

Take, for example, women's workforce participation (the percentage of women who work regularly). Women's workforce participation is far higher in Israel than in the Arab Middle East. Between 2011 and 2015, 58 percent of Israeli women above the age of fifteen were working. In Egypt the number was 24 percent; in Saudi Arabia, 22 percent. Then there is higher education. According to international rankings, there is only one university in the Arab world among the global top three hundred—King Abdulaziz University, a school whose focus is heavily weighted toward the hard sciences and professions. Israel, on the other hand, with 2 percent of the Arab world's population, houses three universities in the top three hundred. Finally, literacy. As of 2015, about 98 percent of Israelis age fifteen or older were literate, as were 95 percent of Turks. That same year, the average literacy rate in the Arab world was 88 percent (in Iran it was 87 percent), with the lowest rate being 69 percent in Morocco.

Whatever the drawbacks in using the totality of the Middle East as a unit of analysis, however, it is important to note that many of the greatest threats to human security affect populations throughout the region, Arab and non-Arab alike. Among those threats are poverty, global warming, environmental degradation, urbanization, and desertification.

How do population pressures affect the Middle East?

There are approximately 510 million people living in the Middle East today—up from 287 million in 1980. Although the rate of growth is declining in the region, the near doubling of the population in a little over thirty-five years has strained available resources and state capacities.

Two factors in particular have added to that strain. First, in the Arab world there is the youth bulge. Just as the millennials—those born between the early 1980s and the late 1990s/early 2000s in the United States—make up the largest generational cohort in American history, their equivalent in the Arab world—those roughly between the ages of ten and twenty-four—is also the largest. The percentage of Arabs between those ages was, in 2014, 29 percent.

In both the case of the millennials and the Arab world's youth bulge, the reason for their numbers is the same: These are the children of baby boomers. In the case of the United States, the baby boom is associated with the return of the GIs from World War II and the prosperity of the 1950s and 1960s. In the Arab world, the baby boom came a bit later, when the interventionist states that emerged during the Period of Decolonization began leaving their mark. The interventionist state brought with it improvements in education, public health, and sanitation. Infant mortality declined, as did the numbers of women who died in childbirth. But there is a downside as well: While being part of a large cohort increased competition among millennials for jobs, housing, services, and the like in the United States, their Arab counterparts have faced even greater challenges as a result of slow economic growth and lower levels of prosperity.

The second factor that has strained resources in the Middle East is urbanization. In 1970, about 42 percent of the inhabitants of the Middle East as a whole lived in urban areas. By

2015, over 60 percent did. The Middle East today is the second most urbanized region in the world (Latin America is the first). And the region not only includes large urban concentrations, but megacities—cities with over ten million inhabitants—as well. For example, Cairo, with about sixteen million inhabitants, ranked as the seventeenth largest city in the world in 2016. Overcrowding and the strain that puts on infrastructure and services are reasons the Egyptian government announced in 2015 a plan to construct a whole new capital city about thirty miles east of the current one. Tehran and Istanbul, each with between thirteen and fourteen million people, share the same problems as Cairo.

Urban growth in the region exceeded total population growth. This indicates that a major factor in this growth has been rural-to-urban migration. The flight of 1.5 million Syrians from the countryside to provincial cities and major urban areas between 2006 and 2010 is just one example of how the push of rural poverty, even without the pull of urban opportunity, has affected the region. The influx of impoverished rural populations into cities throughout the region (the exception here being Israel) has led to what Egyptian sociologist Saad Eddin Ibrahim has called "urbanization without urbanism."[2] For Ibrahim, the "qualitative change in people's outlook, behavioral patterns, and the organizational networks which they create and participate in" is not taking place in the Middle East as a result of urbanization. The result is the expansion of cities devoid of a binding civic culture.

What are the effects of diminishing water supplies on the Middle East?

Although agriculture was invented in the Middle East, the region comprises one of the harshest environments on earth. It is certainly one of the most arid. And that aridity is growing. Increases in population have led to overgrazing, unregulated land use, and soil exhaustion. These, in turn, have led to expanding areas of desert (desertification), which, in 2010, threatened 20 percent of the territory of the entire Middle East. The effects of expanding swathes of parched territory, along with drought and the exhaustion of reserves of fresh water, have already been felt. According to the 2009 Arab Human Development Report, in 1955 three Arab countries out of twenty-two were below the water poverty line; that is, people living in those countries had fewer than fifty liters of water a day—the bare necessity—for drinking, personal hygiene, bathing, and laundry needs. Those countries were Bahrain, Jordan, and Kuwait. By 1990 there were eleven. By 2025, the report predicts that this number will reach eighteen.

Only 43 percent of surface water in the Middle East originates within a single country. This has led to conflict and threats of conflict between states over water rights. For example, in 2011 Ethiopia laid the cornerstone for the Grand Ethiopian Renaissance Dam on the Blue Nile, a tributary of the Nile River. The project, which hearkens back to the colossal infrastructural projects so dear to developmental experts during the early post–World War II period, is expected to provide hydroelectric power to expand electrical production for use in Ethiopia and for sale to Ethiopia's neighbors.

But Ethiopia's downstream neighbor, Egypt, is bitterly opposed to the project. Egyptians fear that it will permanently diminish *their* share of the Nile's waters, vital for Egyptian agriculture. In 2013 the Muslim Brotherhood president of Egypt was even caught discussing creative methods to destroy the dam in a meeting with Egyptian politicians that, unbeknownst to them, was televised. While cooler heads prevailed (and the president was removed anyway in a coup d'état), the dam remains of such concern to the Egyptians that they asked Israel to intervene on their behalf with Ethiopia.

The Egyptian-Ethiopian row was not an isolated incident. Similar conflicts have pitted Turkey against Syria and Iraq, and Israel against its neighbors. The former case also involved the construction of a dam, this time built on the headwaters of the

Euphrates River, which runs through all three countries. The dam's opening in 1990 goaded Syria into funding the PKK in retaliation. In 1964, Israel's unilateral decision to divert what it claimed was its fair share of water from the Jordan River led to a military confrontation with Syria. That confrontation was the first step down a path that eventually led to the 1967 war between Israel and its Arab neighbors. And water remains a bone of contention between Israelis and Palestinians. In 1995, the two sides signed an agreement which divided water from the so-called Mountain Aquifer in the West Bank between the two parties. Israel got 80 percent, the Palestinians the rest. The agreement was to have been revisited in 2000. It never was.

In addition to a lack of water to go around in the region, there is, increasingly, a lack of sufficient supplies of clean water. Poor and unregulated public health practices are partly to blame. For example, according to the World Health Organization, the entire length of the Nile River—the longest river in the world—is polluted by fecal matter. This has not only made it impossible for Egyptians to drink the water without boiling it first, it has bred diseases, including bilharzia. Bilharzia is transmitted through flatworms that breed in infected waters. It causes infertility in women and decreased brain function in children. It is estimated that in rural Egypt approximately 50 percent of the population is infected. Other reasons for the lack of clean water in the region include runoff of chemical fertilizers and pesticides, salinization, and the venality and corruption of governments that allow Europe to use their states as trash receptacles for its waste, much of which is toxic.

What is the impact of war on the environment in the Middle East?

While most analysts of World War I have concentrated on the political, diplomatic, social, and even cultural effects of the war, the great Soviet geochemist, Vladimir Vernadsky (1863–1945), took a decidedly different route. Vernadsky viewed the war as a great geologic event that resulted in, among other things, the accumulation of huge amounts of lead in the soil of battlefields. That lead affected soil fertility, grazing, and water quality. War, in other words, not only takes a human toll, it takes an environmental one as well. And since the Middle East has been the site of more than its fair share of wars, it only stands to reason that war's environmental impact there has been of enormous consequence.

When it comes to war-induced environmental catastrophes, Iraq probably sets the standard. When Saddam Hussein's forces were fleeing Kuwait in 1991, they set upward of 700 oil rigs on fire, prompting talk of climate change caused by smoke blocking out the sun. In addition, there were deliberate and accidental oil spills. Before and during the war, between twenty-five and fifty million barrels of unburned oil flowed from damaged facilities, temporarily making the Persian Gulf an environmental disaster area. Media critics have argued that images of oil-soaked waterfowl on American television were instrumental in mobilizing domestic support in the United States for the war. After the war, Saddam drained the 6,000 square miles of marshland in southern Iraq. He did so to expose Shi'is who fled there after he had put down their rebellion, along with the indigenous (Shi'i) Marsh Arabs, to his wrath. By the time the United States invaded Iraq in 2003, only 7 percent of the marshland remained.

Over the years, much of the marshlands have recovered. But twenty-five years after their near destruction, Iraq became the site of another environmental calamity in the making: the potential collapse of the Mosul Dam as a result of faulty construction and neglect—or even deliberate sabotage. The fear that ISIS would capture the dam and unleash the waters on downriver populations was one of the reasons the Obama administration gave for the American campaign against the group. At the time, it was estimated that should the dam fail, upward of 1.5 million Iraqis might drown in what the American embassy in Iraq called an "inland tidal wave."[3]

How might climate change affect the Middle East?

During summer 2016 the Middle East reached a new milestone: Temperatures in Kuwait rose to the highest point ever recorded on the planet outside Death Valley, California—129.2°F. Kuwait did not broil alone. Temperatures reached 126°F in Iran and Iraq. In fact, the Middle East as a whole was scorching.

Scientists are divided about whether the extremely high temperatures were an aberration or will become the new normal. Some argue that temperature extremes are cyclical and that the temperatures experienced in 2016 were the usual once-in-a-decade spike. Others are less optimistic. Unless climate-warming greenhouse gases are reduced, they argue, Doha, Qatar; Abu Dhabi in the United Arab Emirates; and Bandar Abbas, Iran will reach a felt temperature (combined heat and humidity) of 170°F—the temperature at which human habitation becomes impossible.

While climate change will affect every region of the globe, the Middle East is more vulnerable than most for two reasons. The first has to do with food. The Middle East not only has a high dependence on climate sensitive agriculture, it is dependent as well on agricultural imports from areas that will also be affected by climate change. Scientists predict that higher temperatures and reduced precipitation will increase the occurrence of droughts in the region (it is estimated that an increase of approximately 2°F would reduce available water in Morocco by 10 percent). These droughts have already affected agricultural output and social life in the region, as can be seen from the case of Syria.

Climate change outside the region will likewise diminish the quantity of food available for import. Because of difficult agricultural conditions throughout the Middle East, the region imports more food, particularly grains, than does any other region in the world. Ninety percent of Egyptian wheat, for example, comes from abroad, mostly from Russia. In 2010, wild fires and a heat wave diminished the Russian crop by 40 percent, and Russia took its grain off the international market. Over the course of the following year, food prices in Egypt jumped 30 percent. Scientists have attributed the wild fires and heat wave to climate change.

It would, of course, be simplistic to draw a straight line between the Russian decision to take its grain off the market and the outbreak of the Egyptian uprising a year later. Egyptians harbored multiple grievances against their government. Besides, privation does not necessarily translate into political action. Nevertheless, it is important to remember that alongside the slogan, "The people demand the downfall of the regime," protesters chanted, "Bread, freedom, social justice."

The second reason the Middle East is vulnerable to climate change is that a large proportion of the region's population lives in coastal areas. According to the World Bank, there are forty-three heavily inhabited coastal areas in the region, from Casablanca, Morocco in the west to Bandar Abbas in the east. As temperatures rise and polar ice caps shrink, sea levels rise. Predictions about the effects of rising sea levels on coastal populations are dire: Scientists estimate that a temperature increase of 2° to 5°F would expose six to twenty-five million North Africans to coastal flooding. A half-meter rise in sea levels would displace more than two million inhabitants of Alexandria alone. Rising sea levels would also lead to the further salinization of fresh water sources. Populations that depend on coastal aquifers, such as the population of Gaza, are particularly vulnerable. The 1.5 million inhabitants of the territory depend on a single aquifer, which they share with Israel.

What is the refugee crisis all about?

Before the current refugee crisis, the largest group of refugees in the Middle East was made up of Palestinians who had been displaced during the 1948 and 1967 wars, along with their descendants. There are more than five million Palestinian refugees currently registered with the United Nations High Commissioner for Refugees (UNHCR). Many others are non-registered. Among them are those who have been able to escape life in the refugee camps because they could afford to or because they were able to emigrate abroad. While the rights of Palestinians vary from country to country, only Jordan has offered Palestinian refugees full rights of citizenship (the Jordanian population is divided between those who lived there before 1948 and their descendants—known as "East Bankers"—and Palestinians, who make up a majority of the population).

Now, of course, the attention of the world has shifted to Syrian refugees, particularly those who have sought asylum outside the region. Commentators use the term "refugees" to refer to the Syrians who have left their homes and emigrated abroad deliberately. They differentiate between migrants and refugees. For them, migrants are those who leave their country of origin for economic reasons. Refugees, they maintain, leave for political reasons or because they are fleeing a war zone. In fact, no clear differentiation can be made. Political turbulence frequently leaves economic deprivation in its wake. Furthermore, those who flee one country for political reasons might decamp from their new home for economic ones.

About one million refugees sought asylum in Europe in 2015, and more than 100,000 during the first three months of 2016. Most of these refugees came from camps in the countries that surround Syria. The reason for the surge in emigration to Europe was that the Syrian civil war had dragged on for years, and many of those who had thought of the camps as a temporary refuge simply gave up hope of ever returning to their homes. Others left to escape deepening poverty or an inability to obtain work permits in the countries where they had sought refuge. Still others left because of the lack of educational opportunities for themselves or their children, or because aid shortfalls made their lives in the camps unbearable.

During the 2016 presidential campaign in the United States, much was made of a proposal to ban immigration from Syria until more was known about just who would be immigrating and why. In fact, at the time there was a great deal of information about the refugees. According to statistics gathered by the UNCHR in May 2016, the refugee population was nearly evenly split between men and women. Only about 22 percent were men between the ages of eighteen and fifty-nine—the gender and age range many Americans associate with terrorists. About 56 percent were under the age of seventeen—and 39 percent of those were under eleven. A sampling of refugees in Greece shows that a large number of adults—86 percent—had secondary or university education. Most of them were under thirty-five. Syria is thus losing the very people it will most need if there is to be any hope of rebuilding in the future.

In March 2016 the European Union reached an agreement with Turkey setting the rules for refugees wishing to emigrate from Turkey to Europe. According to the plan, Greece is to return to Turkey all "new irregular migrants" (those not cleared first in camps in Turkey) traveling from Turkey to the Greek islands, where many land. In return, the member states of the European Union promised to allow an equal number of Syrian refugees residing in Turkey to emigrate to Europe. They also promised to boost existing financial support for the refugees still in Turkey. To make the deal even more palatable for the Turks, they agreed to make it easier for Turkish nationals to obtain visas for Europe. International refugee and rights organizations were up in arms. Not only was the agreement inhumane, they argued, it violated European Union and international standards regarding refugees. According to those standards, states could not detain refugees involuntarily and refugees had the right to appeal their deportation.

In addition to a refugee crisis, the Middle East has a related crisis on its hands: The region harbors an unusually high number of internally displaced persons (IDPs), both in Syria and elsewhere. IDPs are people who have left their homes but have not crossed an international border. The Middle East has more IDPs than does any other region in the world. This is, in large measure, the result of the lawlessness that has accompanied state breakdown and the violence of civil wars and foreign interventions (such as the American invasion and occupation of Iraq and the Saudi intervention into Yemen's civil war). According to statistics accumulated between 2014 and 2016, there were 263,500 IDPs in the Palestinian territories (displaced from 1948 through 2014), 417,000 in Libya, upward of 1.2 million in Turkey (many as a result of the Kurdish insurgency and the government's counterinsurgency campaign), 2.8 million in Yemen, and more than four million in Iraq. IDPs have an advantage over refugees because they enjoy the rights of citizenship in their new homes. On the other hand, IDPs frequently lack access to schooling, healthcare, family networks, and employment opportunities. They also suffer disproportionately from depression and post-traumatic stress disorder.

What is the status of women in the Middle East?

The 2005 Arab Human Development Report, titled "Towards the Rise of Women in the Arab World," begins as follows:

> Compared to their sisters elsewhere in the world, [Arab women] enjoy the least political participation. Conservative authorities, discriminatory laws, chauvinist male peers and tradition-minded kinsfolk watchfully regulate their aspirations, activities and conduct. Employers limit their access to income and independence. In the majority of cases, poverty shackles the development and use of women's potential. High rates of illiteracy and the world's lowest rates of female labour participation are compounded to "create serious challenges." Though a growing number of individual women, supported by men, have succeeded in achieving greater equality in

society and more reciprocity in their family and person relationships, many remain victims of legalized discrimination, social subordination, and enshrined male dominance.[4]

Of course, the status and condition of women in the Arab world differ in significant ways from country to country. Saudi women can't drive or travel abroad without the permission of their male guardians, but they can vote in local elections (the only elections there are). Bahraini women are prohibited from working between the hours of 8:00 p.m. and 4:00 a.m. (with some exceptions, such as healthcare providers), but they do have the right to initiate divorce. Nevertheless, according to the World Economic Forum's Gender Gap Report 2015[5] (which ranks countries on the basis of such variables as women's participation in the workforce, literacy, health, and inheritance rights), the Arab world is the worst region on earth to be a woman. The highest-ranking Arab country on its list was Kuwait, which ranked #117 out of the 145 countries surveyed. Yemen came in dead last.

The Middle East is larger than just the Arab world, of course, and Israel did come in at #53 in the rankings, beating out Singapore. Israel, however, was the sole outlier in the region. The ranking for Turkey was #130, two slots below Algeria. Iran came in at #141, only four slots ahead of Yemen. The Arab world was not so out of step with the rest of the region after all.

The subordination of women in the Middle East has played out in a number of ways, from violence against them and child marriage (which, however, is declining) to honor killings (the murder of a female family member for purportedly bringing shame on the family) and female genital mutilation (or FGM—the removal of external female genitalia). Performed to control women's sexuality, FGM is widespread in a number of countries. In 2009, for example, it was estimated that 96 percent of Egyptian women between the ages of fifteen and forty-nine had undergone the "procedure." (That only 23 percent of Yemeni women in the same age range experienced it demonstrates that FGM is a subregional custom, not an Islamic or Arab one.)

Female subordination manifests itself in other ways as well. Although women in all countries in the Middle East have the right to vote (Saudi Arabia, the last on board, bowed to the inevitable in 2011), voting in most of the region is not exactly empowering. Women still lag in participation in governance at the highest levels behind their sisters in every other region of the world (the two exceptions are again Israel and, more recently, Tunisia). And in terms of family issues, most Middle Eastern women are trapped in an entrenched patriarchy. According to a 2013 Pew Research Center Poll, on the average 86 percent of Arabs polled (male and female) believed that a wife must always obey her husband, 63 percent believed family planning was not morally acceptable, and 35 percent believed polygamy morally acceptable. Only 38 percent believed a woman should have the right to divorce her husband and only 26 percent believed that daughters should have equal inheritance rights with their sons.[6]

Most international development agencies agree that economic development hinges on women's participation in the labor force. Unfortunately, female participation in the Arab workforce is about 25 percent—among the lowest in the world. Of course, this number varies from country to country, with the lowest participation in war-torn Syria and Iraq—14 percent and 15 percent, respectively, in 2014. That same year, it was 46 percent in the UAE and 51 percent in Qatar. In addition to entrenched cultural biases against hiring women, women lack employment opportunities in the Arab world because of high reproductive rates, legal systems that make hiring women difficult, and personal status regulations. For example, in some places women need their father's or husband's permission to work. Low female employment means that dependency ratios—the number of dependents each worker supports—are the highest in the world, increasing the numbers of those who live in poverty.

Lack of educational opportunities also hinders women's participation in the workforce. The Arab world also has one of the world's lowest rates of female education (above only sub-Saharan Africa) and, again along with sub-Saharan Africa, the largest gap between male and female education. On the other hand, when women do have access to post-secondary education, they take advantage of it. As of 2012 there were more women than men attending universities in seven Arab countries (as well as in Israel and Iran), although historically the number of women studying technical subjects has been much smaller.

The outlook for women in the Middle East is thus not uniformly bleak, and governments throughout the region have pushed back against women's subordination, with varying degrees of commitment and success. There are three reasons for the pushback. First, it has been in their interest to do so. Secular-minded rulers from Morocco to pre-revolutionary Iran have for years advocated for women as part of their development strategy. They have also used the issue to expand their base of support—and diminish support for oppositional Islamist movements—by reaching out to women and to male liberals. And it did not hurt that their campaigns on behalf of women demonstrated to the outside world the great strides their countries were making and how enlightened their leadership was. Thus, the last shah of Iran appointed his sister honorary head of the High Council of Iranian Women's Associations, and local media dubbed laws expanding women's personal rights in Egypt "Jehan's laws" and "Suzanne's laws" after the presidential wives who purportedly promoted them.

In addition, the logic of neo-liberalism demands a broadening of the marketplace to include the full range of producers and consumers. It is no coincidence that the IMF strongly supports female participation in the labor force, as does Saudi Arabia's "Vision 2030," a neo-liberal roadmap to its core. Although the eighty-six-page document uses the word "women" only five times and is short on details, one of its three highlighted goals is to raise the participation of women in the labor force from 22 to 30 percent in just fourteen years.[7]

In addition to the logic of neo-liberalism, there is another logic at play. Some of the most autocratic leaders in modern times have supported women's rights. This is not because they felt a sudden urge to spread the range of civil liberties available to their populations. That would have been too out of character. Instead, they have supported women's rights because they have sought to expand the reach of the state into the home, and to replace the "private patriarchy" of the husband/father-dominated family with a "public patriarchy" defined by the state. There has been no shortage of autocrats who have used this strategy in the Middle East.

How poor is the Middle East?

Development experts differentiate between "income poverty" and "human poverty." Income poverty focuses on a single variable—the amount of money an individual or household has at its disposal. Human poverty is a more encompassing metric that not only includes income, but takes quality-of-life factors into account as well.

Income poverty is measured in two ways. The first quantifies the number of people living in "extreme poverty." Those who live in extreme poverty have less than $1.90 per day—the international standard—available for expenditures. According to this measure, the Middle East's record is mixed. Those living in extreme poverty in the predominantly Arab part of the Middle East numbered 170 million in 1993 (until 2015, extreme poverty was defined as an income of less than $1.25 per day). That number declined until it reached 107 million in 2010. It then began to climb again, mainly as a result of political instability and conflict. The distribution of those living in extreme poverty is thus unevenly spread across the region. In 2015,

21 percent of Iraqis and 37 percent of Yemenis lived in extreme poverty. On the other hand, the number of citizens of Qatar and the UAE who lived in extreme poverty that year—if there were any—was negligible.

The $1.90 per capita per day measure is not the only way statisticians calculate income poverty. They also go by a country's poverty line, which each country determines for itself based on local conditions. This measure of income poverty is more expansive than the first because it measures all those who live below the national poverty line, not just those who live in extreme poverty.

According to this measure, income poverty in much of the Middle East has been on the rise since the end of the past century. The three main reasons given for the rising numbers of those living below the poverty line in the Middle East are neoliberal policies, which have removed parts of the safety net; high rates of unemployment; and, most significantly, conflict in the Arab parts of the region.

In 2014, sixteen of the twenty-one states in the region registered unemployment rates higher than the international mean of 9.4 percent (only Turkey, Israel, Kuwait, the UAE, and Qatar, in descending order, were below the mean). While there were a number of factors that contributed to those rates, from privatization-induced layoffs to a growth in population that far exceeded the economic growth, one statistic in particular stands out: The Arab world was less industrialized in the first decade of this century than it was in 1970.

Economists cite conflict as the single most important reason that the numbers of those living below the poverty line in the region have spiked since 2010. It has been estimated that as of 2014, 28 percent of Iraqis, 33 percent of Libyans, 38 percent of Gazans, 54 percent of Yemenis, and more than 85 percent of Syrians lived in poverty.

Conflict, however, doesn't explain why the numbers of those living below the poverty line have also increased in those countries in the Arab world that were less affected by protracted violence. Once again, economists cite neo-liberal economic policies, high unemployment, and political turmoil as culprits. But they also cite the low price of oil, which ate into export revenue; the decline in tourism; the aftershock of the spike in food prices; and job nationalization and the substitution of Arab labor by South Asian labor in the Gulf.

In Egypt, the percentage of those living below the poverty line increased one point from 2011 to 2016, reaching 26.3 percent. One percentage point does not seem like much, but it means an increase of upward of one million more Egyptians living in poverty since the outbreak of the uprising there. Even Saudi citizens have been affected by adverse conditions. Sociologists estimate (and estimates are the best that can be had in secretive Saudi Arabia) that in 2015 between 7 and 14 percent of Saudis had at their disposal $17 per day—the poverty line in Saudi Arabia. Income inequality was higher in Saudi Arabia than in Argentina or the United States.

Using the second measure for poverty, high levels of income poverty in the Middle East can also be found outside the Arab world. In 2016, 21 percent of Israelis lived below the poverty line. Although poverty in Israel is usually associated with the Arab and ultra-Orthodox Jewish populations (a sizeable number of ultra-Orthodox men, preferring religious study to work, live off stipends, government handouts, and their wives' salaries), there are increasing numbers of working poor in this category as well. As elsewhere, in Israel neo-liberalism has not been the worker's friend.

It is estimated that 70 percent of Iranians and 40 percent of Turks also live below the poverty line. Economists attribute poverty in Iran mainly to population growth and international sanctions, which began to be lifted only in early 2016. Steps taken by the Iranian government—which oversaw the so-called resistance economy—didn't help either. To counter the sanctions, the government promoted homegrown production to replace imports. The result was the further enrichment of the wealthy and black marketeers in the private sector, as well as agencies owned by the government in the public sector. By 2016, the Islamic Revolutionary Guard Corps reportedly owned a vast majority of Iran's productive capacity.

To explain the rising level of poverty in Turkey, economists point to both a global and domestic economic downturn and the government's pro-natalist (pro-birth) policies. To counter-act the problems associated with a rapidly aging population, the Turkish government has encouraged women to bear three or more children. Unfortunately, neither the Turkish govern-ment nor the Turkish economy can support the increase in family size.

What is the state of human poverty in the non–Gulf Cooperation Council Arab world?

Human poverty is measured by something called a multidi-mensional poverty index, which bases its rankings on three variables: health (as indicated by child mortality and nutri-tion), education (as measured by years of schooling and child enrollment), and standard of living (as measured by access to electricity, clean drinking water, adequate plumbing and sanitation, flooring, cooking fuel, and family assets). While parts of the Middle East measure well in terms of the index, human poverty in non-GCC Arab states has stagnated or has gotten worse.

One of the primary metrics used to measure human pov-erty is life expectancy. Surprisingly, as of 2013 life expectancy throughout the Middle East was higher than the global norm, which was 74.3 years for women and 68.8 years for men. There were four outliers: Yemen, Egypt, and Syria, for both genders, and Iraq, for women. The main causes of deaths in Yemen, Egypt, and Iraq were disease, neonatal complications, and heart disease. In Syria, the main cause was war.

With a few exceptions, such as the reintroduction of polio into Syria and the recent spread of Middle East Respiratory Syndrome (or MERS, which is spread from camels to humans), deaths from contagious diseases have declined in the region. That's the good news. The bad news is that fatalities from non-communicable diseases and injuries are on the increase.

One factor contributing to mortality rates in the Arab world is what the United Nations Development Programme calls "food insecurity." In 2012, for example, there was a 53 percent shortage of grains, 13.5 percent shortage of oil, 8.5 percent shortage of dairy products, and 6.8 percent shortage of sugar in the Arab world. About 10 percent of Arabs were experiencing food shortages—a number that is bound to increase in the future as poverty, climate change, and the effects of political instability and war spread. In 2014, for example, the World Food Programme announced that the percentage of Iraqis, Palestinians, and Yemenis who were undernourished hovered around 30 percent.

The consequences of political instability and war for nutrition in the region have been particularly felt in Syria and Yemen. During the 1990s, Syria produced so much food that it could export the surplus. Then came the 2006–2011 drought. After 2011, things got even worse: Following the outbreak of the uprising, the Syrian government began laying siege to urban areas, using starvation as a weapon. In January 2016, the United Nations estimated that 400,000 people in fifteen separate parts of the country were going hungry. In one town alone (Madaya), twenty-three Syrians starved to death in December 2015.

War had a similar effect on Yemen. Before the Saudi intervention into the Yemeni civil war, Yemen imported 90 percent of the food it needed. Once they entered the war, the Saudis imposed a blockade on Yemeni ports, cutting off food deliveries. As a result, by late summer 2016 the World Food Program classified ten of Yemen's twenty-two provinces as one step away from famine. In the course of a year, the number of Yemeni children at risk from severe acute malnutrition doubled, reaching 320,000.

While most dramatic in Syria and Yemen, the "calorie crisis" in the Arab world can be found in pockets of poverty throughout the region. It is therefore ironic that the region simultaneously suffers from its opposite as well: an obesity epidemic.

The Middle East is the second most obese region in the world (the South Pacific is the first). In 2014, 75 percent of the adult population of Kuwait, Qatar, Libya, Saudi Arabia, and Egypt was overweight (that is, with a Body Mass Index—BMI—of twenty-five or above), and more than a third were obese (BMI of thirty or above). Public health officials point to a number of reasons for the epidemic: the adoption of Western diets, the spread of a different aesthetic (being plump was once a sign of prosperity in the United States, too), and the perpetuation of "traditional roles" and lack of exercise for women. Along with high levels of tobacco use and the highest incidence of traffic accidents per car anywhere, obesity-linked diseases are the most preventable killers in the Arab world. In fact, two diseases linked with obesity—heart disease and diabetes—rank among the most prevalent causes of death in the region.

The sorry state of healthcare and public health services in Arab countries outside the GCC make matters worse. From the 1950s through the 1960s, healthcare and public health improved throughout the region. Investment in healthcare and public health infrastructure had been minimal before the postcolonial republics set the regional standards for state intervention into society. Improvements were therefore not difficult to make. Over time, however, the quality of both declined: Populations grew at faster rates than states' ability to provide for them. The IMF and the neo-liberal doctrines it promoted also constrained states from undertaking large-scale investments, even for the public good.

As a result, healthcare delivery is poor in the Arab world outside the GCC countries. It is inefficient and underfunded, and it lacks skilled personnel. On average, countries in the region spent a little more than 5 percent of their GDP on healthcare in 2014. Compare that to the United Kingdom, which spent 9.1 percent, or the United States, which spent a whopping 17.1 percent (the GCC countries, which have a huge income-to-population ratio, spend proportionately less). And the situation is bound to worsen as populations age. Currently, individuals cover about half of overall healthcare costs by paying out of pocket. This means they have little protection when faced with catastrophic illness or long-term care. It also means that the wealthy receive far better care than those at the middle income level or the poor, those who have no benefits (such as those living in rural areas), and those who do not work for employers legally obliged to provide them with workers' benefits.

What is education like in the Arab world?

The sorry state of healthcare is not the only or even primary reason for the poor showing of Arab countries on the multidimensional poverty index. That honor goes to education. Developmental economists today view harnessing knowledge and innovation in the same way their forebears viewed harnessing steam power: the essential motor for success in a competitive world economy. They even talk of building "knowledge-based economies," which, they claim, will ensure continuous growth and full employment wherever they take root. The key to building a knowledge-based economy is investment in education, which will cultivate workers with research, management, and professional skills.

The history of education in the Arab world is similar to the history of healthcare in the region. Postcolonial states throughout the Arab world promoted free public education on all levels, not only to fulfill their side of the ruling bargain, but also to meet development goals. And it didn't hurt that schools provided a venue for the state to inculcate values and ideologies. In 1960, the literacy rate for all Egyptian adults stood at 26 percent; by 2015, it was 74 percent (which was still below the 85 percent global rate). But literacy is only one metric for rating education. And while literacy is a worthwhile goal in its own right, literacy rates hardly shed light on the quality of education as a whole. As with healthcare, education in the non-GCC Arab world fell victim to rising populations and slow economic growth. The two youth bulges since the early post-colonial period were particularly damaging to the delivery of quality education.

Currently, education in the Arab world, from pre-kindergarten through post-secondary, is notoriously inadequate. According to the 2003 Arab Human Development Report,

> [The] curricula taught in Arab countries seem to encourage submission, obedience, subordination and compliance, rather than free critical thinking. In many cases, the contents of these curricula do not stimulate students to criticise political or social axioms. Instead, they smother their independent tendencies and creativity.[8]

Whether schools in the Arab world can change remains to be seen. Schools educate not only by *what* they teach, but *how* they teach. In other words, values held in high regard outside the classroom—such as open debate, creativity, and cooperation in democratic societies—are reproduced and practiced in the classroom setting. Autocratic and highly patriarchal societies prize none of those values which, in turn, are the essential building blocks of a knowledge-based economy.

Twenty-first century education in the Arab Middle East is structurally incapable of promoting debate or critical thinking. Rote memorization is encouraged and only memorization and factual recall are tested. Universities other than foreign branch campuses or universities registered elsewhere (such as the American University in Cairo and the American University in Beirut) are under the direct control of the government. They tend to be overcrowded as a result of free tuition, the youth bulge, and neo-liberal budget cutting. They are also staffed by instructors who often are hired and promoted on the basis of political loyalty rather than on the basis of competence. In a number of Arab countries, professors have had to belong to the ruling party. And because they tend to earn meager salaries, they cannot devote themselves fully to teaching and research.

The inadequacies of universities in the Arab world are one of the reasons the GCC countries encourage university-age youths to study abroad. It is also one of the reasons those youths are eager to do so. In 2015, 60,000 Saudi students enrolled in American universities alone (because of low oil prices, which forced Saudi Arabia to cut scholarship benefits, that number will probably decline in coming years). Still, sending students abroad is hardly an adequate way to jump-start knowledge-based economies—particularly since 95 percent of Arab youths who study abroad do not return home.

Can human security be measured?

In 2000, member states of the United Nations adopted a set of eight "Millennium Development Goals" to be met by the international community during the first fifteen years of the new century. Those goals were as follows:

1. "Eradicate extreme poverty and hunger."
2. "Achieve universal primary education."
3. "Promote gender equality and empower women."
4. "Reduce child mortality."
5. "Improve maternal health."
6. "Combat HIV/AIDS, malaria, and other diseases."
7. "Ensure environmental sustainability."
8. "Develop a global partnership for development."[9]

To ensure the international community and its various regions made progress meeting these goals, agencies affiliated with the United Nations set specific targets that might be quantified (in the case of the Arab world, that agency was the Economic and Social Commission for Western Asia). For example, there were three targets for goal #1, including "halve, between 1990 and 2015, the proportion of people whose income is less than US$1.25 a day." For goal #7 there were four, including "halve, by 2015, the proportion of people without sustainable access to safe drinking water and basic sanitation." And for goal #8 there were also four, including "deal comprehensively with the debt problems of developing countries through national and international measures in order to make debt sustainable in the long term." In sum, there were nineteen targets.

According to a progress report published in 2013,[10] the Arab world was doing a poor job hitting those targets. Of the nineteen, the Arab world was on the path to hitting only three of them: gender parity in primary and secondary education, HIV/AIDS treatment, and the use of new technologies, particularly information and communications technology. The Arab world was on the path to failing to hit eight targets; the results so far in another eight were a mixed bag.

There is reason to believe that human security in the Arab world is in even worse state than the 2013 progress report suggests. For example, the targets themselves are idiosyncratic. True, protecting biodiversity is important, but what about human rights and political participation, both of which are also components of human security? Neither was included in the 2013 progress report (although the authors of the report recommend their inclusion in the future). In addition, because the targets had to be quantitatively measureable, the data ignored qualitative analysis. It is one thing to measure gender parity in schools or the number of women in parliament. But what about the quality of those schools, or the fact that however many women serve in parliaments in the Arab world, those parliaments are rarely the final arbiter of the law?

Finally, whatever the problems in data collection and analysis, the 2013 progress report was unfortunately timed—as the report itself discusses. Since the report's publication, political, social, and economic conditions in much of the region have deteriorated to an extent that will not be fully understood for years.

In light of these factors, and of the report's own finding, it is difficult to characterize human security in the Arab world as on the path to progress. Indeed, the region's trajectory seems to be moving in the opposite direction.

What are the greatest threats to human security in the New Middle East?

Middle Easterners face a myriad of challenges that directly affect human security in the region. Some of these challenges are connected to deep-seated practices.

For example, economists draw a direct link between women's workforce participation and education, on the one hand, and national economic development, on the other. Nevertheless, patriarchal values embedded in the family and political institutions ensure women are disadvantaged in both.

Adult male Yemenis enjoy socializing and chewing qat during their siestas. The leaves of the qat plant contain a stimulant whose affect is somewhat like a double espresso. Yemen, a country in the midst of water and food crises of epic proportions, uses about 40 percent of the water available for agriculture for irrigating its inedible qat crop. (Lest Americans feel smug, it should be noted that during the 2011–17 California drought—the greatest in over a century—the state produced 71 percent of America's head lettuce, often used as a garnish for burgers and sandwiches. Lettuce has little caloric value. Waste is in the eyes of the beholder.)

Some threats to human security in the Middle East are less associated with deep-seated social practices. Perhaps the two threats of this sort that loom the largest are what is euphemistically called the "lack of good governance" and the pitiable state of most economies in the region.

The region as a whole measures poorly in terms of corruption, repression, accountability, transparency, democratic practice, respect for the rule of law, and concern for human rights. From Iran's "Green Revolution," which broke out in response to the stolen presidential election of 2009, to the Arab uprisings and social protest movements in Israel (2011) and Turkey (2013), populations took their frustration and anger to the streets with varying degrees of success. In some places, states responded by warring on them. In others, states lost the ability to ensure public safety. In still others, states called for or opened themselves up to foreign intervention. The result region-wide has been a decrease in human security and a rise in human poverty, both directly and indirectly. In terms of the latter, the uprisings enabled ISIS to gain a foothold in the region and sparked a massive refugee crisis.

The effects of poor governance will continue to spin themselves out in the immediate future. How can regimes that cannot rule effectively or win the support of their populations possibly deal with emerging crises such as those brought on by population growth, climate change, or water and food shortages?

Similar questions might be raised with regard to the problem of the region's economies. A region in which most states have not been able to wean themselves from dependence on rent is not one likely to prosper in a world that gives pride of place to free markets and the cultivation of each state's comparative advantage. Just what finished products might most Middle Eastern states produce better and more cheaply than other states in the global market? Setting aside such fanciful ideas as building the knowledge-based economies of the future and habituating populations to the free market, how will it be possible to halt the economic free fall that has devastated parts of the region? How will it be possible to ratchet up performance in economies that are now treading water?

Condoleezza Rice's New Middle East got off to a rocky start. Its prospects have not improved with time.

What might the recent history of the Middle East teach us about the possibility of overcoming the lack of good governance?

The term "Arab Spring" obscures the true nature of the wave of uprisings that began in 2010. Rather than representing an isolated and short-term phenomenon, they are the culmination of decades-long agitation for human and democratic rights and social and economic justice in the region. Placing recent events in this context demonstrates that, in spite of recent setbacks, those rights and that concept of justice have become something of a lodestar that has guided large numbers of politically minded Middle Easterners for years. There is no reason to believe, therefore, that the current lack of good governance in the region will necessarily remain a permanent state of affairs.

Large-scale protests and uprisings for human and democratic rights began in the region in the early 1980s. Many of them were cross-sectarian or nonsectarian. Many included a broad coalition of Islamists, liberals, trade unionists, and leftists.

The demand for human rights lay at the heart of the "Berber Spring" of 1980, the fight by Algeria's largest ethnic minority for its rights. Eight years later, the Algerian "Black October" riots led to the first democratic elections in the Arab world (unfortunately, the government overturned their results). The Bahraini *intifada* of 1994–99 began with a petition signed by one-tenth of Bahrain's inhabitants demanding an end to emergency rule, the restoration of rights revoked by that rule, release of political prisoners, pardons for political exiles, and the expansion of the franchise to women ("intifada" is Arabic for "shaking off," and is now commonly used to mean rebellion). Petitioners also demanded a restoration of the 1973 constitution, which provided for a parliament in which two-thirds of the members were to be elected.

The death of Syrian dictator Hafez al-Assad in 2000 spawned the rise of political salons throughout Syria. Participants in those salons expanded their movement through the circulation of the "Statement of the Ninety-nine," then the "Statement of a Thousand," which echoed many of the same demands made during the Bahraini intifada, along with demands for multiparty elections and freedom of speech, assembly, and expression. Even after the "Damascus Spring" turned into the

"Damascus Winter," aftershocks of the mobilization continued. Among those aftershocks was the Damascus Declaration Movement of 2005, which (initially) united the secular and religious opposition in a common demand for democratic rights.

These movements were only the tip of the iceberg. Following the spread of the pro-democracy *diwaniyya* (civic council) movement in the wake of the expulsion of Iraqi troops from Kuwait in 1991, Kuwait experienced two "color revolutions." The first—the "Blue Revolution"—lasted from 2002 to 2005. It won for Kuwaiti women the right to vote. A year later, Kuwaitis organized the "Orange Revolution" to promote electoral reform. In 2004, secular and Islamist Egyptians banded to form a group called "Kefaya" ("Enough"), which called on Mubarak to resign. In Morocco, popular agitation led to the establishment of the Equity and Reconciliation Commission in 2004 to investigate human-rights abuses that had occurred during the previous thirty years—the so-called Years of Lead. Lebanese took to the streets in 2005 in their Cedar Revolution, demanding the withdrawal of Syrian forces from that unfortunate country and parliamentary elections free from Syrian interference. In 2004, 2008, and 2010 Kurdish citizens protested for minority rights in Syria. And the list goes on.

Alongside these protests and uprisings for human rights and democratic governance were protests and uprisings for social and economic justice. Beginning in the late 1970s with IMF riots, this agitation continued through a six-month general strike in the Gafsa phosphate-mining region of Tunisia in 2008, and the surge of Egyptian labor activism from 2004 through 2010. During that period of activism, two million Egyptian workers and their families participated in more than 3,000 strikes, sit-ins, and walkouts. Sometimes protesters framed their demands in class terms; at other times, they framed them in human rights terms, as in the 2011 Tunisian slogan, "A job is a right."

The protests and uprisings of 2010–11 amplified these earlier protests and uprisings in two ways. First, by combining demands for human and democratic rights with demands for social and economic justice, they involved a much broader segment of the population wherever they broke out. Second, they were more widespread. Uprisings unfolded in near simultaneity across national boundaries until they engulfed almost the entirety of the Arab world.

Recent protests have not been confined just to the Arab world. In the wake of the Iranian presidential elections of 2009, which the incumbent "won" with more than 60 percent of the vote and which supporters of his opponents charged he had stolen (in seventy cities the number of votes exceeded the number of eligible voters), protests broke out throughout Iran. Within two days, crowds estimated at anywhere between one and three million participated in a mass rally in Tehran. Tens of thousands more took to the streets in other cities as well. As the protests continued, the regime cracked down hard, deploying paramilitary thugs to beat up protesters. It also ordered mass arrests and the torture of those whom it had imprisoned. Nevertheless, thousands of Iranians returned to the streets of Tehran two years later to demonstrate their solidarity with Tunisians and Egyptians—and to protest autocracy closer to home.

In Turkey, protesters occupied Gezi Park in the heart of Istanbul in spring 2013 to protest government plans to demolish the park and build in its stead a shopping mall. As protests in Turkey spread to over ninety cities, the issues at stake expanded as well. Of particular concern to many protesters was what they perceived to be the growing authoritarianism and high-handedness of Prime Minister Erdogan. Many also feared the growing Islamization of institutions and laws at the hands of the ruling Islamist party.

Not even Israel has been immune. In 2011, after having been evicted from her apartment, a twenty-five-year-old video editor pitched a tent in Habima Square, Tel Aviv, and opened a Facebook page to spread the word about her plight. Others soon joined her. As had happened in Turkey, what had begun as a campaign against a single issue—the high cost of housing—soon turned into a more generalized protest against government policy. Of particular concern was expanding poverty, government corruption, the widespread gap between rich and poor, and the imposition of American-style neo-liberal economic policies—the same sort of social justice issues that inspired protests throughout much of the rest of the world during that season of discontent.

The breadth and depth of the protests and uprisings that have engulfed the Arab world, Iran, Turkey, and Israel indicate that agitation for good governance is not a transient or localized phenomenon in the Middle East. As such, the history of the past thirty years cannot but disturb the sleep of politicians, kings, and dictators throughout the region.

NOTES

Preface

1. Peter Catterall, "What (if Anything) is Distinctive about Contemporary History," *Journal of Contemporary History* 32 (October 1997), 450.
2. William Faulkner, *Requiem for a Nun* (New York: Vintage International, 2011), 73.

Chapter 1

1. *World Population Prospects, the 2015 Revision* (New York: United Nations Department of Economic and Social Affairs, Population Division, 2016), https://esa.un.org/unpd/wpp/Download/Standard/Population/ (last accessed March 28, 2017).
2. *Democracy Index 2010: Democracy in Retreat* (London: Economist Intelligence Unit, 2010), https://graphics.eiu.com/PDF/Democracy_Index_2010_web.pdf (last accessed March 28, 2017).
3. Nathan J. Brown, *When Victory Is Not an Option: Islamist Movements in Arab Politics* (Ithaca, NY: Cornell University Press, 2012), 1.
4. *Arab Human Development Report 2004: Towards Freedom in the Arab World* (New York: United Nations Development Programme, 2004), http://hdr.undp.org/en/content/arab-human-development-report-2004 (last accessed March 28, 2017).
5. "Remarks by President George W. Bush at the Twentieth Anniversary of the National Endowment for Democracy" (Washington, DC: National Endowment for Democracy, 2003), http://www.ned.org/remarks-by-president-george-w-bush-at-the-20th-anniversary/ (last accessed March 28, 2017).

6. Condoleezza Rice, "Remarks at the American University in Cairo" (Washington, DC: US Department of State, 2005), https://2001-2009.state.gov/secretary/rm/2005/48328.htm (last accessed March 28, 2017).

7. Jason Brownlee, *Democracy Prevention: The Politics of the U.S.-Egyptian Alliance* (Cambridge, UK: Cambridge University Press, 2012).

8. William R. Brown, "What Sadat's Assassination Means to America," *Christian Science Monitor*, October 14, 1981, http://www.csmonitor.com/1981/1014/101425.html (last accessed March 28, 2017).

9. "Secretary Rice Holds a News Conference," *Washington Post*, July 22, 2006, http://www.csmonitor.com/1981/1014/101425.html (last accessed March 28, 2017).

10. Richard N. Haass, "The New Middle East," *Foreign Affairs* (November–December 2006), https://www.foreignaffairs.com/articles/middle-east/2006-11-01/new-middle-east (last accessed January 27, 2017).

Chapter 2

1. "Statistics reveal casualties since military coup in Egypt," *Middle East Monitor*, February 5, 2014, https://www.middleeastmonitor.com/20140205-statistics-reveal-casualties-since-military-coup-in-egypt/ (last accessed March 28, 2017).

2. Francine Kiefer, "Obama on Egypt: Praise for the 'Moral Force of Nonviolence,'" *Christian Science Monitor*, February 11, 2011, http://www.csmonitor.com/Commentary/Editorial-Board-Blog/2011/0211/Obama-on-Egypt-Praise-for-the-moral-force-of-nonviolence (last accessed March 28, 2017).

3. "Court Clears Seven Policemen Accused of Killing Protesters in 2011 Uprising," *Egypt Independent*, May 22, 2013, http://www.egyptindependent.com/news/court-clears-seven-policemen-accused-killing-protesters-2011-uprising (last accessed March 28, 2017).

4. See James T. Quinlivan, "Coup-Proofing: Its Practice and Consequences in the Middle East," *International Security* 24 (Autumn 1999), 131–65.

5. "GYBO Manifesto 2.0," Gaza Youth Breaks Out, n.d., https://gazaybo.wordpress.com/about/ (last accessed January 27, 2017).

Chapter 3

1. *Freedom in the World 2010* (Washington, DC: Freedom House, 2010), https://freedomhouse.org/report/freedom-world/freedom-world-2010 (last accessed March 29, 2017).

2. "Corruption Perceptions Index 2010" (Berlin: Transparency International, 2010), http://www.transparency.org/cpi2010/results (last accessed March 31, 2017).

3. *Human Development Report 2010: The Real Wealth of Nations* (New York: United Nations Development Programme, 2010), hdr.undp.org/sites/default/files/reports/270/hdr_2010_en_complete_reprint.pdf (last accessed March 29, 2017).

4. *Arab Human Development Report 2004: Towards Freedom in the Arab World* (New York: United Nations Development Programme, 2004), http://hdr.undp.org/en/content/arab-human-development-report-2004 (last accessed March 28, 2017).

5. Anne Bernard, "As Syria's Revolution Sputters, a Chaotic Stalemate," *New York Times*, December 27, 2014, http://www.nytimes.com/2014/12/28/world/as-syrias-revolution-sputters-a-chaotic-stalemate.html (last accessed January 27, 2017).

6. Jennifer Cafarella, "Syrian Opposition Guide" (Washington, DC: Institute for the Study of War, October 7, 2015), http://understandingwar.org/backgrounder/syrian-opposition-guide (last accessed March 29, 2017).

7. Thomas L. Friedman, "Obama on the World: President Obama Talks to Thomas L. Friedman About Iraq, Putin and Israel," *New York Times*, August 8, 2014, https://www.nytimes.com/2014/08/09/opinion/president-obama-thomas-l-friedman-iraq-and-world-affairs.html (last accessed March 29, 2017).

8. "Syria: Abductions, Torture and Summary Killings at the Hands of Armed Groups" (London: Amnesty International, July 5, 2016), https://www.amnesty.org/en/latest/news/2016/07/syria-abductions-torture-and-summary-killings-at-the-hands-of-armed-groups/ (last accessed March 29, 2017).

9. Malik al-Abdeh, "Rebels, Inc.," *Foreign Policy*, November 21, 2013, http://foreignpolicy.com/2013/11/21/rebels-inc/ (last accessed January 27, 2017).

10. "Syria Confronting Fragmentation! Impact of Syrian Crisis Report" (N.P.: Syrian Centre for Policy Research, February 2016), www.ara.cat/2016/02/11/1520927894.pdf?hash (last accessed March 29, 2017).

11. http://scpr-syria.org/publications/policy-reports/confronting-fragmentation/ (last accessed January 27, 2017).
12. Amr Salahi, "The Evacuation of Homs: Humanitarianism or Ethnic Cleansing?" *Middle East Monitor*, March 29, 2014, https://www.middleeastmonitor.com/20140329-the-evacuation-of-homs-humanitarianism-or-ethnic-cleansing/ (last accessed January 27, 2017).

Chapter 4

1. Graeme Wood, "What ISIS Really Wants," *Atlantic*, March 2015, http://www.theatlantic.com/magazine/archive/2015/03/what-isis-really-wants/384980/ (last accessed January 27, 2017).
2. "Statement by the President on ISIL," September 10, 2014, https://obamawhitehouse.archives.gov/the-press-office/2014/09/10/statement-president-isil-1 (last accessed March 29, 2017).
3. "From Hijrah to Khilafa," *Dabiq 1: The Return of the Khilafah*, Ramadan 1435 (July 2014), https://clarionproject.org/docs/isis-isil-islamic-state-magazine-Issue-1-the-return-of-khilafah.pdf (last accessed January 27, 2017).
4. Jessica Stern and J.M. Berger, "ISIS and the Foreign Fighter Phenomenon," *Atlantic*, March 8, 2015, https://www.theatlantic.com/international/archive/2015/03/isis-and-the-foreign-fighter-problem/387166/ (last accessed April 2, 2017).
5. Dahlia Lithwick, "Scalia v. Scalia,"*Atlantic*, June 2014, https://www.theatlantic.com/magazine/archive/2014/06/scalia-v-scalia/361621/ (last accessed March 29, 2017).
6. Lisa Stampnitzky, *Disciplining Terror: How Experts Invented "Terrorism"* (New York: Cambridge University Press, 2013), 147.
7. "Welcome to the Islamic State Land," September 9, 2014, http://www.military.com/video/operations-and-strategy/terrorism/welcome-to-the-islamic-state-land/3775821940001 (last accessed March 29, 2017).
8. "ISIS Use Top Video Game Grand Theft Auto 5 to Recruit Children and Radicalise the Vulnerable," *Daily Mail*, September 22, 2014, http://www.dailymail.co.uk/news/article-2765414/Isis-use-video-game-Grand-Theft-Auto-5-recruit-children-radicalise-vulnerable.html#ixzz4cknIQhzu (last accessed March 29, 2017).
9. Daniel Byman, "ISIS Goes Global: Fight the Islamic State by Targeting its Affiliates," *Foreign Affairs*, March/April 2016, https://www.foreignaffairs.com/articles/middle-east/isis-goes-global (last accessed March 29, 2017).

10. David Remnick, "Going the Distance: On and Off the Road with Barack Obama," *New Yorker*, January 27, 2014, http://www.newyorker.com/magazine/2014/01/27/going-the-distance-david-remnick (last accessed March 29, 2017).

11. Jeffrey Goldberg, "The Obama Doctrine," *Atlantic*, April 2016, http://www.theatlantic.com/magazine/archive/2016/04/the-obama-doctrine/471525/ (last accessed January 27, 2017).

Chapter 5

1. Turki al-Feisal, "Mr. Obama, We Are Not 'Free Riders,'" *Arab News*, March 14, 2016, http://www.arabnews.com/columns/news/894826 (last accessed January 27, 2017).

2. "Iranian President Cites Late Ayatollah as Saying Jewish State 'Must Be Wiped from the Map of the World,'" *CNN Wire*, October 27, 2005, http://www.cnn.com/2005/US/10/26/wednesday/ (last accessed March 30, 2017).

3. *The Iraq Inquiry*, July 6, 2016, http://www.iraqinquiry.org.uk/the-report/ (last accessed January 27, 2017).

4. George W. Bush, "Address to a Joint Session of Congress and the American People," September 20, 2001, https://georgewbush-whitehouse.archives.gov/news/releases/2001/09/20010920-8.html (last accessed March 30, 2017).

5. Scott Wilson and Al Kamen, "Global War on Terror is Given New Name," *Washington Post*, March 25, 2009, http://www.washingtonpost.com/wp-dyn/content/article/2009/03/24/AR2009032402818.html (last accessed March 30, 2017).

6. "President Obama's Inaugural Address," January 21, 2009, https://obamawhitehouse.archives.gov/blog/2009/01/21/president-barack-obamas-inaugural-address (last accessed March 30, 2017).

7. Jeffrey Goldberg, "The Obama Doctrine."

8. *2016 World Press Freedom Index* (Paris: Reporters Without Borders, 2016), https://rsf.org/en/ranking (last accessed March 30, 2017).

Chapter 6

1. *Arab Human Development Report 2009: Challenges to Human Security in the Arab Countries* (New York: United Nations Development Programme, 2009), http://www.arab-hdr.org/PreviousReports/2009/2009.aspx (last accessed March 28, 2017).

2. Navtej Dhillon and Amina Fahmy, "Urban and Young: The Future of the Middle East" (Washington, DC: Brookings Institution, June 11, 2008), https://www.brookings.edu/

opinions/urban-and-young-the-future-of-the-middle-east/ (last accessed January 27, 2017).

3. Keith Johnson, "U.S. Warns of 'Catastrophic Failure' of Iraq's Mosul Dam," *Foreign Policy*, February 29, 2016, http://foreignpolicy.com/2016/02/29/u-s-warns-of-catastrophic-failure-of-iraqs-mosul-dam/ (last accessed March 30, 2017).

4. *Arab Human Development Report 2005: Towards the Rise of Women in the Arab World*, (New York: United Nations Development Programme, 2005), hdr.undp.org/sites/default/files/rbas_ahdr2005_en.pdf (last accessed March 28, 2017).

5. *The Global Gender Gap Report 2015* (Geneva: World Economic Forum, 2015), www3.weforum.org/docs/GGGR2015/cover.pdf (last accessed March 30, 2017).

6. *The World's Muslims: Religion, Politics, and Society* (Washington, DC: Pew Research Center's Forum on Religion & Public Life, 2013), http://www.pewforum.org/2013/04/30/the-worlds-muslims-religion-politics-society-women-in-society/ (last accessed March 30, 2017).

7. "Full Text of Saudi Arabia's Vision 2030," *al-Arabiya English*, April 26, 2016, https://english.alarabiya.net/en/perspective/features/2016/04/26/Full-text-of-Saudi-Arabia-s-Vision-2030.html (last accessed March 30, 2017).

8. *Arab Human Development Report 2003: Building a Knowledge Society* (New York: United Nations Development Programme, 2003), hdr.undp.org/sites/default/files/rbas_ahdr2003_en.pdf (last accessed March 28, 2017).

9. *The Arab Millennium Development Goals Report: Facing Challenges and Looking beyond 2015* (New York: United Nations Development Programme, 2014), http://www.arabstates.undp.org/content/rbas/en/home/library/MDGs/arab-states.html (last accessed March 28, 2017).

10. *The Arab Millennium Development Goals Report.*

FURTHER READING

General works on the Middle East

Beinin, Joel. *Workers and Peasants in the Modern Middle East*. Cambridge, UK: Cambridge University Press, 2001.

Cammett, Melani and Ishac Diwan. *A Political Economy of the Middle East*. 4th ed. Boulder, CO: Westview, 2015.

Gelvin, James L. *The Modern Middle East: A History*. 4th ed. New York: Oxford University Press, 2016.

Topical Books

Allan, Tony. *The Middle East Water Question: Hydropolitics and the Global Economy*. London: I.B. Tauris, 2002.

Arab Human Development Report 2009: Challenges to Human Security in the Arab Countries. New York: United Nations Development Programme, 2009. http://www.arab-hdr.org/contents/index.aspx?rid=5 (last accessed March 28, 2017).

Beinin, Joel. *Workers and Thieves: Labor Movements and Popular Uprisings in Tunisia and Egypt*. Stanford, CA: Stanford University Press, 2015.

Bunzel, Cole. "From Paper State to Caliphate: The Ideology of the Islamic State." Washington, DC: Center for Middle East Policy at Brookings, March 2015. https://www.brookings.edu/research/from-paper-state-to-caliphate-the-ideology-of-the-islamic-state/ (last accessed April 19, 2016).

Chollet, Derek. *The Long Game: How Obama Defied Washington and Redefined America's Role in the World*. New York: PublicAffairs, 2016.

Di Giovanni, Janine. *In the Morning They Came for Us: Dispatches from Syria*. New York: Liveright, 2016.

Einhorn, Robert. "Debating the Iran Nuclear Deal." Washington,
    DC: Brookings Institution, August 12, 2105. https://www.brookings.
    edu/series/debating-the-iran-deal/ (last accessed April 19, 2016).
Gelvin, James L. *The Arab Uprisings: What Everyone Needs to Know.* 2nd
    ed. New York: Oxford University Press, 2015.
Gerges, Fawaz. *ISIS: A History.* Princeton, NJ: Princeton University
    Press, 2016.
Goldberg, Jeffrey. "The Obama Doctrine." *Atlantic,* April 2016. http://
    www.theatlantic.com/magazine/archive/2016/04/the-obama-
    doctrine/471525/ (last accessed January 27, 2017).
Haas, Mark L., and David W. Lesch, eds. *The Arab Spring: The Hope and
    Reality of the Uprisings.* 2nd ed. Boulder, CO: Westview, 2016.
Lesch, David W. *Syria: The Fall of the House of Assad.* New Haven,
    CT: Yale University Press, 2012.
Lynch, Marc. *The New Arab Wars: Uprisings and Anarchy in the Middle
    East.* New York: Public Affairs, 2016.
Matthiesen, Toby. *Sectarian Gulf: Bahrain, Saudi Arabia, and the Arab
    Spring That Wasn't.* Stanford, CA: Stanford University Press, 2013.
Owen, Roger. *The Rise and Fall of Arab Presidents for Life.* Cambridge,
    MA: Harvard University Press, 2012.
Phillips, Christopher. The *Battle for Syria: International Rivalry in the New
    Middle East.* New Haven, CT: Yale University Press, 2016.
"The Politics of Sectarianism." POMEPS Studies 4. Washington,
    DC: Project on Middle East Political Science, November 13, 2013.
    https://pomeps.org/2013/11/14/the-politics-of-sectarianism/ (last
    accessed April 19, 2016).
Swain, Ashkok, and Jägerskog, Anders. *Emerging Security Threats in the
    Middle East: The Impact of Climate Change and Globalization.* Lanham,
    MD: Rowman & Littlefield, 2016.
Worth, Robert H. *A Rage for Order: The Middle East in Turmoil, from Tahrir
    Square to ISIS.* New York: Farrar, Straus, and Giroux, 2016.

Websites

The Conversation (wide-ranging content from academics and
    researchers). https://theconversation.com/us.
Foreign Policy. www.foreignpolicy.com.
International Crisis Group. www.crisisgroup.org.
Jadaliyya (Ezine of the Arab Studies Institute). www.jadaliyya.com.
al-Jazeera (English version of popular Arab newspaper based in Qatar).
    http://english.aljazeera.net.

Middle East Research and Information Project (MERIP). http://www.merip. org.

al-Monitor (reports by journalists based in the Middle East). http://al-monitor.com/pulse/home.html.

Project on Middle East Political Science (POMEPS). https://pomeps.org/.

Syria Comment (blog of Syria expert Joshua Landis). http://www. joshualandis.com/blog/.

Wikileaks. https://wikileaks.org/.

INDEX

al-Abadi, Haidar, 128
Abbas, Mahmoud, 135–136
Aden, 6
Afghanistan
    expansion of ISIS to, 97
    Soviet Union invasion of, 84, 87
    US invasion of, 85, 109, 121–122
Africa, expansion of ISIS to, 97
Ahmad, Muhammad, 91
Ahrar al-Sham (Free Men of
    Syria), 49, 65, 69–70, 71, 91–92
Alawites, 4, 42, 58, 59, 60, 61, 77–79
al-Assad, Bashar, 18, 42, 57, 67, 68,
    70, 118
al-Assad, Hafez, 57, 61, 164
Alevis, 4, 77
Algeria
    Berber Spring, 39, 164
    Black October, 164
    demographics of, 8
    expansion of ISIS to, 97
    independence of, 6–7
    ISIS defeats in, 108
    Islamist parties, 37
    as postcolonial republic, 14
    relations with Turkey, 134
    status of women in, 149
Amnesty International, 70

Anarchist movements,
    37–38, 111
Apocalyptic vision, 88–90
Apostates, defined, 88
April 6 Youth Movement, 25, 46
Arab Human Development
    Reports (UNDP), 141, 159
    *The Challenges to Human Security
    in the Arab Countries*, 137
    *Towards the Rise of Women in the
    Arab World*, 148–149
Arabic language, 3
Arab League, 128
Arab News, al-Faisal letter to
    Obama, 116–117
Arabs, 2, 3
Arab Spring, use of term, 27–29,
    163–164
Arab uprisings, 22–23
    in Bahrain, 26, 41–43, 44, 49
    in Egypt, 25, 29, 32, 33–36, 47, 49
    events leading to, 24–27
    in hybrid democracies, 45–46
    impact of, 48–49, 165–167
    Islamic movements and, 37–39
    in Libya, 26, 27, 28–29, 32,
    39–41, 48, 49
    in monarchies, 43–45

Arab uprisings (*contd.*)
   reasons for failure of, 47–48
   region-wide factors for, 29–33
   in Syria, 26, 28–29, 32,
      41–43, 48, 49
   in Tunisia, 24–25, 32, 33–35, 49
   in Yemen, 25–26, 28–29,
      39–41, 48, 49
Army of Conquest. *See* Jaysh al-
   Fatah (Army of Conquest)
Army of Islam. *See* Jaysh al-Islam
   (Army of Islam)
Asia
   expansion of ISIS to, 97
   Obama attempt to pivot
      toward, 121

Baba Sheikh, 98
al-Baghdadi, Abu Bakr, 85,
   87–90, 109
Bahrain
   colonial structures
      embedded in, 14
   demographics of, 8
   independence of, 6
   intifada in (1994–99), 164
   religions in, 3
   status of women in, 149
   uprising in, 26, 41–43, 44, 49
Baker, James, 121
Barrel bombs, 58, 70, 73
Battle of the Camel, 36
Benefits for compliance pact,
   10–11, 29–30
Berbers, 2, 27, 39, 164
Bilharzia, 142
bin Ali, Zine al-Abidine, 24–25
bin Laden, Osama, 84–85, 86, 114,
   121–122
"Black hole states," 12–13
Boko Haram, 97, 105, 108
Bouazizi, Muhammad, 24
Brahimi, Lakhdar, 81
Bremer, Paul, 85–86

British Royal Geographic
   Society, 1
British Royal Navy, 18
Bush, George W., 120, 121
   Freedom Agenda, 15–16
   Global War on Terrorism
      (GWOT), 18, 122

Caliphate (*khalifa*), defined, 87
Carter, Jimmy, 16–17
Catholics, 3
Caucasus, expansion of ISIS
   to, 97
Chechens, 109
Child soldiers, of ISIS, 108
China
   Crusader-Zionist Conspiracy
      and, 87
   oil prices and, 125–126
Christians
   ISIS taxation of, 100
   in Middle East, 3
   as target of ISIS, 98, 106
Climate change, 56, 143, 144–145
Clinton, Bill, 114
Coalition Provisional Authority
   (CPA), Iraq, 85–86
Cold War, 17, 22, 112, 117–118, 124
Copts, 3
Crony capitalism, 30, 56
Crusader-Zionist
   Conspiracy, 87
Cubs of the Caliphate, 108

Dabiq (ISIS magazine), 89, 91–92
Daesh (al-Dawla al-Islamiya fi
   al-'Iraq wal-Sham). *See* Islamic
   State in Iraq and Syria (ISIS)
Day of Rage, 26, 28, 46
Deep state, defined, 34
Democracy Index (EIU), 11–13
Demographics, 2–4, 32, 139–140.
   See also specific countries
Denmark, 110

Desertification, 141
Disease. *See* Public health issues
Drones, 107, 123
Druze, 4, 78

Economic development, 8–9, 17, 150
Economist Intelligence Unit, Democracy Index, 11–13
Education, 151, 158–160
Egypt
    as black hole state, 12–13
    censuses in, 2
    demographics of, 8, 32
    expansion of ISIS to, 97, 105
    foreign aid, 9
    and IMF, 29
    income poverty, 154
    independence of, 5
    Islamist parties, 37
    Kefaya group, 165
    labor activism, 165
    oil exports, 19
    as postcolonial republic, 14
    as pro-Soviet during 1960s, 113
    relations with Turkey, 133
    religions, 3
    status of women in, 149–150, 151
    uprising in, 25, 29, 32, 33–36, 47, 48, 49
    urbanization, 140
    water rights issues, 141, 142
Egyptian Centre for Economic and Social Rights, 34
Ennahda, 34–35, 39
Environmental pollution, 142, 143–144
Erdogan, Recep Tayyip, 119–120, 132, 134, 166
Ethiopia, Grand Ethiopian Renaissance Dam, 141
European Union
    emigration to, 146, 147

Turkey's ambition for membership, 132
Extreme poverty, 152

al-Faisal, Turki (Prince), 116
Farsi, 3
Female genital mutilation (FGM), 149–150
Food imports and prices, 33, 48, 144–145, 154
Food insecurity, 156–157
Foreign aid, 9–10
France
    Period of Decolonization, 6
    support for autocracies, 14
    Sykes-Picot Agreement, 4–5
Freedom House, *Freedom in the World* report (2010), 54–55
Free Men of Syria. *See* Ahrar al-Sham (Free Men of Syria)
Free rider problem, 115–116
Free Syrian Army (FSA), 69, 91–92, 102
Friends of Syria group, 63
Front for Victory in [Greater] Syria. *See* Jabhat Fateh al-Sham (Front for Victory in [Greater] Syria)
Future Movement, Lebanon, 128

Gaza
    income poverty, 153
    uprising in, 46
Gaza Youth Breaks Out, 46
GCC. *See* Gulf Cooperation Council (GCC)
Georges-Picot, François, 4
Global War on Terrorism (GWOT), 18, 41, 122–123
Global warming. *See* Climate change and human security
Great powers. *See* United Kingdom (UK); United States (US)

Greater Middle East. *See headings at* Middle East
Greater Syria, use of term, 84
Greece, emigration agreement with Turkey, 147
Guest workers, 2, 8, 19–20, 127, 154
Gulf Cooperation Council (GCC), 40, 115, 127, 130, 133
Gulf War (1991), 20, 114, 143
GWOT. *See* Global War on Terrorism (GWOT)

Haass, Richard N., 21–22
Hamas, 129–130
Harakat Ahrar al-Sham al-Islamiyya. *See* Ahrar al-Sham (Free Men of Syria)
Healthcare. *See* Public health issues
Hebrew, 3
Higher Negotiations Committee (HNC), 79
Hijra (migration of Muslims), 88, 105
Hisba (ISIS police force), 99
Hizbullah, 21, 43, 61, 62 74, 76, 119, 128
Holy sanctuaries (Mecca/Medina), 114
Houthis, 40–41, 116, 121, 128
Human poverty, in non-GCC Arab states, 155–158
Human Rights Revolution, 30–31
Human security, in New Middle East, 137–167. *See also* Refugee crisis
climate change, 143, 144–145
education, 151, 158–160
environmental damage due to war, 142–144
good governance and, 161–167
human poverty in non-GCC Arab countries, 155–158

human security, defined, 137–139
income poverty, 152–155
Millennium Development Goals, 160–162
population pressures, 139–140
status of women, 138, 148–152, 162
threats to, 137, 162–163
water resources, 140–142
Hussein, Saddam, 8, 77, 85–86, 114, 132, 143
Hybrid democracies, 12, 13, 45

Ibadis, 4
Ibrahim, Saad Eddin, 140
IMF. *See* International Monetary Fund (IMF)
Income poverty, in New Middle East, 152–155
India
Bharatiya Janata Party, 38
Crusader-Zionist Conspiracy and, 87
Ink spot strategy, of ISIS, 97, 107–108
Institute for the Study of War, 68–69
Internally displaced persons (IDPs), 147–148
International Labor Organization, 75
International Monetary Fund (IMF)
and diversification in GCC states, 126–127
income reports, 8
labor protests against, 30, 165
neo-liberal economic policies, 8–9, 11, 29–30, 33, 55–56
support for women in workforce, 151
International relations, of New Middle East, 112–136. *See also specific countries*

Israel-Palestine conflict, 118–119,
    134–136
    Obama administration and,
        112–125
    role of oil, 125–127
    roots of Saudi-Iranian rivalry,
        127–132
    Turkey's new role, 130, 132–134
Iran
    as ally of Syria, 61–62
    and Arab uprisings, 131
    as authoritarian regime, 13
    autocratic structures, 14
    coup in (1953), 18
    demographics of, 2, 8
    Green Revolution (2009), 166
    impact of climate change
        on, 144
    income poverty, 154–155
    intervention in Syria, 43
    Kurds, 2
    Obama policy toward, 124–125
    oil production and lower prices,
        125–126
    P5 + 1 nuclear deal with, 119,
        124–125, 129
    as postcolonial republic, 15
    religions, 3, 4
    rivalry with Saudi Arabia, 48,
        68, 80, 106, 113, 127–132
    Shi'i Islam, 3
    status of women in, 151
    as threat to Israel/Saudi
        Arabia, 119
    US dual containment policy, 114
    US invasion of Iraq and, 114
Iran-Iraq War (1980–88), 114
Iraq
    Baath Party, 85–86
    collapse of army (2014), 93, 109
    environmental pollution,
        143–144
    formation of, 5

as hybrid democracy, 12, 13, 45
    impact of climate change
        on, 144
    impact of Syrian civil war on,
        74, 76–77
    independence of, 5
    internally displaced persons
        (IDPs), 148
    ISIS and, 105, 107
    ISIS caliphate in, 99–100
    Kurds, 2, 74, 79, 102–103
    Mosul Dam, 143–144
    oil production, 126, 133
    as postcolonial republic, 14
    poverty, 152–153
    relations with Kuwait, 8
    religions, 3, 4, 46, 77, 85,
        86, 93–94
    status of women in, 150
    Sunni demonstrations, 77
    uprisings in, 45–46, 48–49
    US dual containment policy, 114
    US invasion of, 22, 76, 84, 85–86,
        87, 93, 114, 121–122
ISIS. See Islamic State in Iraq and
    Syria (ISIS)
Islam. See Shi'i Islam; Sunni Islam
Islam for Dummies, 96
Islamic Front, 68–69
Islamic movements, popularity
    of, 37–39
Islamic Revolutionary Guard
    Corps, 62, 155
Islamic State in Iraq (ISI), 70
Islamic State in Iraq and Syria
    (ISIS), 23, 35, 41, 48, 83–111
    apocalyptic vision
        controversy, 88–90
    beliefs of, 83, 86–88, 105
    comparison to al-Qaeda, 88, 96,
        107, 110
    divisions within, 108-109
    expansion of, 96–97

Islamic State in Iraq and Syria
  (ISIS) (*contd.*)
    formation of, 43, 49, 60, 77, 84–86
    genocidal policies, 83
    global terrorist attacks by, 83,
      103–105, 110
    ground victories of, 91–94, 96
    impact on region, 105–106
    life under caliphate, 98–101,
      106–109
    name origins, 83–84
    potential outcomes, post-
      caliphate, 109–111
    recruitment, 94–96
    Syrian ceasefire negotiations
      and, 79–80
    Syrian civil war and, 64–65, 68,
      70, 74
    US efforts against, 101–103
Islamic State of Iraq and the
  Levant (ISIL), 83, 85
Islamist, defined, 37
Israel
    as ally of US, 113
    boundaries, 7
    conflicts with Lebanon, 21
    Crusader-Zionist Conspiracy
      and, 87
    as flawed democracy, 12
    formation of, 5
    income poverty, 154
    independence of, 6
    intervention in Syria, 74
    Israel-Palestine conflict, 118–119,
      134–136
    neo-liberalism in, 11
    official languages of, 3
    opposition to Iran nuclear deal, 119
    protests in (2011), 166–167
    relations with Saudi Arabia, 136
    relations with Turkey, 133–134
    religions, 3–4
    rent income, 10
    settler movement, 119, 120
    status of women in, 149

    wars with Arab states, 136, 142
    water rights issues, 142
Italy, 6, 40

Jabhat al-Nusra (Support Front),
    49, 60, 70, 71, 79–80, 91, 110
Jabhat Fateh al-Sham (Front for
    Victory in [Greater] Syria), 60,
    65, 70, 116
Jaysh al-Fatah (Army of
    Conquest), 70
Jaysh al-Islam (Army of Islam), 65
Jihadi, use of term, 60
Job nationalization, 20, 154
Jordan
    as ally of US, 113
    as authoritarian regime, 12
    colonial structures
      embedded in, 14
    formation of, 5
    impact of Syrian civil
      war on, 74
    Islamist parties, 37
    Palestinian refugees in, 146
    refugees from Syria, 75
    religions, 4
    and Syrian opposition, 66
    uprisings in, 44–45
Judaism, 3–4

Kennedy, John F., 113
Kerry, John, 80, 122
Khalifa. See Caliphate (*khalifa*),
    defined
Khalifa family, 42
Kharajites, 90
King Abdulaziz University, 138
Koran for Dummies, The, 96
Kurdish, 55
Kurdish People's Protection Units
    (YPG), 68
Kurdish Regional Government
    (Iraq), 133
Kurds
    in Iraq, 2, 74, 79, 102–103

as stateless nationality, 39
in Syria, 55, 65–66, 74, 107, 165
as target of ISIS, 87, 98, 106
in Turkey, 2, 77
Kuwait
as authoritarian regime, 12
Blue/Orange Revolutions, 165
British support for, 8
colonial structures
embedded in, 14
demographics of, 8
environmental disasters, 143
impact of climate change on, 144
independence of, 6
oil exports, 9
religions, 3
status of women in, 149, 165
uprising in, 43–44

Labor groups, 38. *See also specific
unions and groups*
protests against IMF, 30, 165
in uprisings, 26, 32, 36,
46, 53–54
League of Nations, mandates
system, 5
Lebanon
Cedar Revolution (2005), 165
censuses in, 2
colonial structures
embedded in, 14
demographics of, 8
formation of, 5
as hybrid democracy, 12, 13, 45
impact of Syrian civil war on,
75–76
independence of, 6
Israeli invasion (2006), 21
refugees from Syria, 75–76
religions, 3, 4
Saudi support for, 128
Taif Agreement (1989), 19
uprising in, 45, 48–49
US interventions in, 113–114
Liberal internationalists, 115

Libya
as authoritarian regime, 13
Berber role in uprisings, 27
demographics of, 32
Government of National
Accord, 41
income poverty, 153
independence of, 6
internally displaced persons
(IDPs), 148
ISIS defeats in, 107–108, 109
ISIS expansion to, 97
ISIS impact on, 105
as postcolonial republic, 14
relations with Turkey, 133
UN formation of, 6, 40
uprising in, 26, 27, 28–29, 32,
39–41, 48, 49
as weak state, 39–40
Life expectancy, 155
Literacy rates, 138

"Make American great
again," 38
Makhlouf, Rami, 56
al-Maliki, Nouri, 93, 109, 128
MANPADS (man-portable air-
defense systems), 64–65
March 15 Youth Movement, 46
Maronites, 3
Marxism, 37–38
McKinsey & Co., 127
Middle East (1945–2011), 1–23. *See
also* Human security, in New
Middle East; *specific countries*
boundaries and state system
of, 4–11
demographics of, 2–4
exploitation of oil, 18–21
formation of
autocracies, 12–18
New Middle East concept, 21–23
political culture of, 11–13
Western support for
autocracies, 15–18

Middle East, use of term, 1–2
Middle East and North Africa
    (MENA). *See headings at*
    Middle East
Middle East Respiratory
    Syndrome (MERS), 155–156
Militaries
    Egypt, 34, 36, 41, 54
    Iran, 166
    Libya, 33
    support for autocracies by, 17
    Tunisia, 54
    UAE, 41
    Yemen, 26, 33, 40
Military Operations Command
    (MOC), 66
Millennials, 139
Millennium Development Goals,
    160–162
Morocco, 39
    colonial structures
        embedded in, 14
    Equity and Reconciliation
        Commission, 165
    independence of, 6
    Islamist parties, 37
    uprising in, 26, 43–44
    Years of Lead, 165
Mubarak, Hosni, 15–16, 18, 25, 35,
    36, 62, 118, 165
Muhammad (prophet), 38, 88, 129
Multidimensional poverty index,
    155, 158
Muslim Brotherhood (Egypt), 34,
    36, 39, 117, 133
Muslim Brotherhood
    movements, 130
Muslims. *See* Islam and Muslims
Mutually hurting stalemate, 67–68

National Coalition for Syrian
    Revolutionary and
    Opposition Forces. *See*

Syrian National
    Coalition (SNC)
National Endowment for
    Democracy, 15
Nativism, defined, 37–39
NATO. *See* North Atlantic Treaty
    Organization (NATO)
Near East. *See headings at*
    Middle East
Neoconservatives, 115
Neo-liberalism
    application in Middle East, 11
    definition, 10
    as factor in Arab uprisings,
        29–31, 33
    and healthcare, 157
    and income poverty, 153–154
    origins, 11
    protests against, 166–167
    in Vision 2030 plan for Saudi
        Arabia, 127, 151–152
Netanyahu, Benjamin, 119
New Middle East, use of term, 21
New Ottomanism, 132–133
Nigeria, expansion of ISIS to, 97
9/11, 114, 122
North Africa, impact of climate
    change on, 145
North Atlantic Treaty
    Organization (NATO),
    41, 121

Obama, Barack
    Arab uprisings and, 36, 62, 68
    efforts against ISIS, 101–103
    on ISIL, 90
    Middle East strategy under,
        112–115, 120–125, 131–132
    policy toward Iran, 124–125
    relations with partners, 116–120
Obesity, 157
Oil exports and prices, 9, 17, 18–21,
    101, 125–127, 154

Oman
    British support for, 8
    colonial structures
        embedded in, 14
    religions, 4
    uprising in, 43–44
Orthodox Christians, 3
Oslo Accord, 134–135
Ottoman Empire, 4, 132–133

Pakistan, expansion
        of ISIS to, 97
Palestine, 39
    formation of, 5
    as hybrid democracy, 12, 13, 45
    internally displaced persons
        (IDPs), 148
    Islamism in, 37, 129–130
    refugee crisis and, 145–146
    relations with Israel, 134–136
    UN recognition of, 7
    uprisings in, 46
    water rights issues, 142
Palestine Liberation
        Organization (PLO),
        113–114, 134–135
Peoples' Protection Units (YPG),
        102, 106–107
Period of Decolonization, 6–10,
        40, 139
Peshmerga, 102, 106–107
Pew Research Center, 150
Polio, 72–73, 155
Pollution. See Environmental
        pollution
Portugal, 6
Post-traumatic stress disorder,
        73, 148
Privatization, 30, 56, 153
Proxy wars, 68. See also Syrian
        civil war
Public health issues, 72, 142, 155,
        156–158

Public patriarchy vs. private
        patriarchy, 151–152
Putin, Vladimir, 62, 66–67

Qaddafi, Muammar, 13, 18,
        40, 115
al-Qaeda, 49, 60, 70
    comparison to ISIS, 88, 96,
        107, 110
    Crusader-Zionist Conspiracy
        concept, 87
    in Iraq, 84–85, 109
    al-Qaeda Central, 86–87
    US policies and, 122–123
Qatar
    absence of uprising in, 41
    colonial structures
        embedded in, 14
    demographics of, 2
    income security, 8, 153
    independence of, 6
    lack of uprisings, 43
    and Saudi Arabia, 129
    status of women in, 150
    support for Syrian opposition,
        63, 69–70
Qur'an, 38, 99
al-Qurayshi al-Hashimi, Caliph
        Ibrahim, 88

Radicalization model, 95–96
Radio Free Europe/ Radio
        Liberty, 94
RAND Corporation, 95
Refugee crisis, 74–76, 77, 105, 106,
        145–148
Religion, in Middle East, 3.
        See also specific religions
Rent, 9–10, 20–21
Reporters Without Borders, 127
Revolutionary wave, use of
        term, 27–28
Rice, Condoleezza, 15–16, 21

Ripeness theory, 67–68
Russia. *See also* Soviet Union, former
    as ally of Syria, 61, 62–63, 66–67
    impact of climate change
        on, 145
    intervention in Syria, 43
    relations with Turkey, 134
    Crusader-Zionist Conspiracy
        and, 87

al-Sadat, Anwar, 16–17
Sahrawis, 39
Salafism, 38, 60, 83, 116. *See also*
    Islamic State in Iraq and
    Syria (ISIS)
Saleh, Ali Abdullah, 18, 40, 41
Salman, Muhammad bin, 127
Saud, Abdulaziz ibn, 5
Saud, Muhammad ibn, 90–91
Saudi Arabia
    and Arab uprisings, 43–44
    as authoritarian regime, 12
    autocratic structures, 14
    expansion of ISIS to, 97
    export of Wahhabism, 117
    formation of, 5, 6–7
    as free rider, 116–117
    income inequality, 154
    intervention in Bahrain, 26, 43
    intervention in Yemen, 41
    Obama and, 116, 118
    oil exports, 9, 126
    as partner of US, 113
    practive foreign policy, 131–132
    relations with Israel, 136
    religions, 3, 130–131
    rivalry with Iran, 48, 68, 80, 106,
        113, 127–132
    status of women in, 151–152
    support for jihadis in
        Afghanistan, 84
    support for Syrian opposition,
        49, 63, 65, 66, 69–70

US Lend-Lease assistance to, 17
US troops in, 114
Vision 2030, 127, 151–152
Saudi Aramco, 127
Scalia, Antonin, 94
Sectarianism, 3, 48–49, 73, 76–77,
    129–130
    in Bahrain, 42
    in Iraq, 45
    in Lebanon, 13
    in Syria, 42, 59, 73–74
Sectarianization, 48, 59–60, 93,
    105–106
al-Shabab, 105
Shi'is/Shi'i Islam
    in Iraq, 46, 76–77, 85, 86
    origins of, 3, 129
    in Saudi Arabia, 130–131
    as target of ISIS, 87, 88, 98
SNC. *See* Syrian National
    Coalition (SNC)
Social media, 25, 28
Social personality disorders, 96
Somalization of Syria, 81
Southern Front, 64–65, 69
Soviet Union, former. *See*
    also Russia
    collapse of, 22
    invasion of Afghanistan, 84, 87
    and Cold War in Middle
        East, 112
Spain, 6
Starvation, 49, 72, 74, 156
Sunni Islam
    in Bahrain, 42–43
    in Iraq, 46, 76–77, 86, 93–94
    origin of, 3
Support Front. *See* Jabhat al-Nusra
    (Support Front)
Sykes, Mark, 4
Sykes-Picot Agreement
    (1916), 4–5, 7
Syria

Arab uprisings and, 26, 28–29, 32, 41–43, 49
Baath Party, 54, 55
coups, 17
Damascus Declaration Movement (2005), 165
Damascus Spring/Winter (2000), 57, 164–165
elite cohesion in, 41–43, 54, 59
emergency law, 52–53
expansion of ISI to, 99–100
foreign aid to, 9–10
formation of, 5
Freedom House report (2010), 54–55
impact of ISIS, 105
income poverty, 153
independence of, 6, 17
Kurdistan Workers' Party (PKK) and, 142
Kurds, 2, 55, 65–66, 74, 107, 165
map of, 50
as postcolonial republic, 14
religions, 4
social market economy, 55–56
status of women in, 150
2015 government offensive, 107
urbanization, 140
water rights issues, 142
"Syria Confronting Fragmentation! Impact of Syrian Crisis Report," 71–72
Syrian Centre for Policy Research (SCPR), 71–73
Syrian civil war, 51–81. See also Refugee crisis; specific groups
beginning of, 26, 51–53
casualties and damage, 71–74
comparison to uprisings in Tunisia/Egypt, 53–54
foreign support for government, 61–63, 67
foreign support for opposition, 49, 63–66, 69–70, 74, 90
impact on neighboring countries, 74–77
militarization of uprising, 57–59
opposition fighters, 68–71
potential outcomes, 77–81
public health, 72–74
sectarianism and, 48
sectarianization of uprising, 59–60
Syrian Democratic Forces, 102
Syrian Islamic Front, 68
Syrian Islamic Liberation Front, 68
Syrian National Coalition (SNC), 63–64, 79
Syrian Network for Human Rights, 70
Syrian Revolution 2011 against Bashar al-Assad group, 52
Syriatel, 56

Taif Agreement (1989), 19
Takfir, 88,
Taliban, 38, 108, 109
Tamazight, 2, 39
al-Tawhid wal-Jihad, 84–85
Transparency International, 54
Trump, Donald, 90, 120, 132
Tunisia
Arab uprisings and, 24–25, 32, 33–35, 49
demographics of, 32
Gafsa strike (2008), 165
impact of ISIS, 105
independence of, 6
Islamist parties, 37
as postcolonial republic, 14
uprising in, 24-25, 32, 41, 48, 49
women, 150
Tunisian General Labor Union (UGTT), 24, 53–54

Turkey
    autocratic drift, 119
    autocratic structures in, 14
    creation of, 5–6
    demographics of, 2, 8
    emigration agreement with
        EU, 147
    Gezi Park protests (2013), 166
    as hybrid democracy, 12, 13
    impact of Syrian civil war on, 77
    income poverty, 154–155
    internally displaced persons
        (IDPs), 148
    and ISIS, 100, 101, 107
    Justice and Development
        Party, 132
    Kemalism, 132
    Kurdistan Workers' Party
        (PKK), 66, 134
    Kurds, 2, 65, 74, 77, 80, 97, 107,
        120, 165
    neo-liberalism in, 11
    refugees from Syria, 75
    relations with US, 119–120
    religions, 3, 4
    role in New Middle East, 130,
        132–134
    status of women in, 149
    support for Syrian opposition,
        63, 65–66, 70, 74, 90, 120
    Iraqi oil, 133
Turkish language, 3

UGTT. See Tunisian General Labor
        Union (UGTT)
UNHCR. See United Nations High
        Commissioner for Refugees
        (UNHCR)
UNDP. See United Nations
        Development
        Programme (UNDP)
Unemployment, 32, 56, 76, 153–154
United Arab Emirates (UAE)
    absence of uprising in, 43

colonial structures
    embedded in, 14
income security, 153
independence of, 6
intervention in Bahrain, 43
oil exports, 9
status of women in, 150
United Kingdom (UK)
    colonial legacy, 6
    decline of influence in region, 16
    healthcare expenditures, 157
    Sykes-Picot Agreement, 4–5
    support for autocracies,
        7–8, 14, 18
United Nations (UN)
    formation of Libya, 40
    Geneva III negotiations, 125
    Millennium Development
        Goals, 160–162
    Palestinian statehood, 7, 46,
        135–136
    Regional Bureau for Arab
        States, 59
    role in decolonization, 6
    Security Council resolutions, 63
United Nations Development
        Programme (UNDP), 56, 137,
        156. See also Arab Human
        Development
        Reports (UNDP)
United Nations High
        Commissioner for Refugees
        (UNHCR), 75, 146, 147
United Nations Population
        Division, 2
United States (US). See also specific
        presidents and agencies
    and Arab uprisings, 47, 68, 118,
        121–122
    and Crusader-Zionist
        Conspiracy, 87
    dual containment policy, 114
    efforts against ISIS, 101–103, 106,
        107, 120, 143–144

energy independence, 126
foreign aid to Israel, 10
Global War on Terrorism
    (GWOT), 18, 41, 122–123
Gulf War (1991), 20, 114, 143
healthcare expenditures,
    157–158
interventions in Lebanon,
    113–114
invasion of Afghanistan, 85, 109,
    121–122
invasion of Iraq, 22, 76, 84,
    85–86, 87, 93, 114, 121–122
neo-liberalism and, 10–11, 31
offshore balancing, 112–115
P5 + 1 nuclear deal with Iran,
    119, 124–125, 129
predominance in region, 16–17
relations with Turkey, 119–120
support for autocracies,
    7–8, 17–19
support for economic
    development, 9
support for jihadis in
    Afghanistan, 84
support for Syrian opposition,
    63, 64–66
and Syrian refugees, 75
Urbanization, 139–140
US State Department
    list of terrorist organizations, 69
    "Run—Don't Walk—to ISIS
    Land" (video), 95
US Treasury Department, 101
Utopianism, defined, 37

Vernadsky, Vladimir, 142–143

al-Wahhab, Muhammad ibn
    'Abd, 90–91
Wahhabism, 38, 117

Weak states, 39
Wilayat, 97, 99–100
Women, status of, 138, 148–152,
    162, 165
World Bank, 9, 145
World Economic Forum, Gender
    Gap Report (2015), 149
World Food Programme, 156
World Health Organization,
    72, 142

Yarmouk Martyrs Brigade, 64
Yazidis, 4, 87, 94, 98, 102, 106
Yemen, 6
    average adjusted income rates, 8
    civil war and food
        insecurity, 156
    Egyptian/Saudi proxy war, 113
    expansion of ISIS to, 97
    extreme poverty in, 152–153
    foreign aid, 19
    impact of ISIS, 105
    income poverty, 153
    internally displaced persons
        (IDPs), 148
    ISIS defeats in, 108
    Islamist parties, 37
    as postcolonial republic, 14–15
    qat, 162
    religions, 3, 4
    Saudi-led intervention, 41, 116,
        121, 148, 156
    status of women in, 149
    unification of South/North, 6, 7
    uprising in, 25–26, 28–29,
        39–41, 48, 49
    as weak state, 39–40

al-Zarqawi, Abu Musab,
    84–85, 86, 88
Zaydis, 4, 41